THOMAS COOK OF LEICESTER

by
Robert Ingle

edited by
Judith Loades

HEADSTART HISTORY

© **ROBERT INGLE 1991**

All rights reserved. No production, copy or transmission of this publication may be made without written permission. No paragraph of this publication may be reproduced, copied or transmitted save with written permission or in accordance with the provisions of the Copyright Act 1956 (as amended). Any person who does any unauthorised act in relation to this publication is liable to criminal prosecution and civil claim for damages.

Published by	HEADSTART HISTORY
	PO Box 41, Bangor, Gwynedd LL57 1SB
Set by	LAZERTYPE
	Bridgegate Pavilion, Chester Business Park
	Wrexham Road, Chester CH4 9QH
Printed by	THE IPSWICH BOOK COMPANY LTD
	The Drift, Nacton Road,
	Ipswich, Suffolk IP3 3QR

ISBN 1 873041 16 0
A CIP catalogue record for this book is available from the British Library

Front Cover : Thomas Cook Printed by kind permission
of Thomas Cook Archives

ACKNOWLEDGEMENTS

Particular thanks are due

To: Edmund Swinglehurst, the archivist at THOMAS COOK Ltd. - for the opportunity to research copies of *The Excursionist* family letters and other documents, and for his generous help and encouragement.

To: Tom Budge who placed his considerable collection of Thomas Cook memorabilia at my disposal together with the valuable and expert information on the nineteenth century Baptist Church.

To: The Leicester County Libraries Leicester Collection.

To: To the Leicester Records Office for the opportunity to research the Baptist Church Minutes Book and other documents.

To: The Goldsmiths Library at London University copies of Thomas Cook's early Temperance publications.

To: The University of Leicester Library's excellent Transport History Collection.

I would like to record my personal thanks to Roderick Boyd of the Ipswich Book Company and to Suzanne Brown of LazerType, Chester.

CONTENTS

Introduction

Prologue

I	Early Years	1
II	The Railways Come to Leicester	13
III	Thomas Cook Moves to Leicester	25
IV	Thomas Cook goes to Europe	25
V	Expansion	37
VI	New Frontiers	43
VII	Family Matters	55
	Epilogue	65
	Bibliography	67

INTRODUCTION

Thomas Cook is a household name around the world so it is an honour for me to publish THOMAS COOK OF LEICESTER in this important year. As a student at the University many years ago I soon discovered how proud Leicester is of its connection with this great man.

It has been a pleasure to read and edit Robert Ingle's book. He is, of course, well known in Leicester for his eloquent and convincing portrayal of Thomas Cook, a role which he first enacted in 1983 to launch the conference brochure for the University of Leicester. The idea was the inspiration of Robert's wife, Sue, the Conference Manager to the University. Since then Robert has appeared as Thomas Cook on many occasions throughout Britain and will have an important part to play in the festival in July 1991.

Robert Ingle taught history until 1982 and since then has devoted his time to researching the life and work of Thomas Cook. Formal acknowledgements are noted elsewhere but a special debt is noted here to Sue Ingle by the author, for the idea and continuing encouragement, and by the publisher, for providing the opportunity to produce this book and in doing so give the people of LEICESTER a chance to read about the "father of modern travel".

Judith Loades
Bangor, June 1991

"Mr. C. has had the merit of entering into an enterprise, which has proved the means of affording pleasure and improvement to thousands of persons, who, but for that enterprise, would never have visited many interesting scenes and places, and improved their minds by acquiring much useful knowledge".

The Leicester Chronicle 1850

PROLOGUE

On July 18th, 1892, Thomas Cook suffered a stroke and died. A few days later the funeral cortege of Leicester's most famous citizen made its way through the gates of the Welford Road Cemetery where he was buried close to the Midland Railway that had played such an important part in the development of his travel empire. Buried with him were his wife, Marianne, who had died before him in 1884 and his daughter, Annie Elizabeth, who had died tragically in 1880. Not until recent years, when an open marble book was added which included the words "HE BROUGHT TRAVEL TO THE MILLIONS", did the inscription contain any reference to his work.

The Funeral Service and later the Memorial service were held at Archdeacon Lane Baptist Church, Leicester, where he had worshipped for many years. Leicester's redevelopment has since demolished all trace of the church but present at both of those services was a young lad, Albert H. Bishop, the son of the officiating minister and some time later, in August, 1952, he wrote of his memories of the funeral in a letter to the Reverend Thomas Budge, then Baptist Minister of Melbourne, Derbyshire.

"I remember well the service," he wrote. "Everything in the church that could be draped in black was so draped including the pulpit. The chapel was crowded. I have now no real remembrance of the matter of the sermon my father preached on that occasion but it was delivered amid a silence that betokened so intense an interest as to be almost painful."

A leading article in *The Times* of July 20th, 1892 referred to Thomas Cook and his son as "the Julius and Augustus Caesar of the modern travel business". Prophetically it stated that his "name ... is likely to be preserved from oblivion for many a day", and noted that Thomas Cook was typical of the Victorian middle class who had raised themselves by their own efforts from small beginnings.

I
EARLY YEARS

Thomas Cook was born in a labourer's cottage on November 22nd, 1808, in Quick Close, Melbourne, Derbyshire, the only son of John and Elizabeth Cook. His father died when Thomas was only four, and in the same year his mother married again to a Mr. James Smithard and further children were born to her, one of them, Simeon Smithard, later becoming a troublesome apprentice to Thomas in Market Harborough, Leicestershire.

His mother's family name was Perkins and his grandfather was Thomas Perkins. He came from Hinckley, Leicestershire, and was an early convert of the evangelistic revival which centred on the village of Barton-in-the-Beans, Leicestershire. Although Thomas' mother could neither read nor write she clearly perceived the value of schooling as far as her son was concerned for Thomas later recorded that he had three diligent schoolmasters, naming them as Mr. Pickering, Rev. John Smith and Mr. Joseph Tagg. Aged ten, Thomas was sent to work for a market gardener named Robey for a penny a day - a much-needed salary with his step-father's death. Since his employer drank heavily, young Thomas frequently found himself solely responsible for hawking the produce of the market garden in the neighbouring villages and this gave him good experience. In 1822 it was decided that Thomas should cease his connection with market gardening and become indentured to his uncle John, a cabinet-maker.* This lasted around five years and must have been successful for we see him later in Market Harborough taking on his own apprentice wood-turners.

Joseph Foulkes Winks came into Thomas Cook's life in 1824. He arrived at Melbourne to become minister of the General Baptist Church just before Thomas Cook's 16th birthday. He was a charismatic man of many talents. The effect on the small Derbyshire Town must have been electric and all the evidence shows that his

---

*John Pegg came from a leading family of General Baptists in Melbourne, his mother is reputed to have sold her wedding-ring in 1768 to help in providing funds for the enlargement of the chapel, but this did not prevent her son from some over-indulgence in liquour. One again Thomas Cook had come up against the effects of strong drink and it is possible that his thoughts were already being exercised by the problems of heavy drinking.

ministry was generally successful. Such a personality was not to be contained within Melbourne and he spent much time away. Finally it was decided that unless he could spend more time attending to his pastoral duties he would have to leave. His influence on the adolescent Thomas Cook was considerable and it was during Wink's pastorate that Thomas was baptized by total immersion on February 28th, 1826.

Joseph Winks was spending so much of his time away from his duties at Melbourne because he was becoming increasingly involved with printing and publishing. In Melbourne he had set up a printing press in a room over a granary owned by John Earp, a close friend of Thomas Cook. (Joseph Winks moved to Leicester in 1830, set up his printing press in High Street and continued to be publisher to the General Baptist Association.)

About 1827 Thomas Cook's apprenticeship with Uncle John came to an end and he assisted his mother in opening the retail shop in her small home. The merchandise of earthenware and books seems a strange combination. The sale of books in the illiterate Elizabeth Perkins little shop in her cottage is probably explained by her son's friendship with Joseph Winks who must have been anxious to find any outlet for his publications. There is no record of how long the shop continued and the revenue from it could not have gone very far in feeding three children and Elizabeth Perkins herself.

Thomas Cook's church activities were highlighted by a somewhat curious (and convoluted) entry in the Melbourne Baptist Church Minute Book for October 20th, 1828 which reads: "it was agreed that Brother Nailor shall send a letter to the committee of the Home Mission on behalf of Brother Cook, as a recommendation, so far as regards his piety - and as a suitable person for the important work of an Evangelist, so far as we judge him fit, what other qualifications are requisite we as a Church not knowing the extent of the work devolving on a person in that station, we leave the case to the discretion and Judgment of the committee". In "November 18th, 1828 came Thomas Cook a young man to be employed in reading the scripture and distributing tracts in the neighbourhood". There was some opposition to such a young man though a little success is noted. Whatever kept Thomas Cook going it could not have been the monetary reward. He commenced his labours at a salary of £36 per year. Which in 1829 was reduced to £26. The reason put forward was that he received many presents from the people. This diminution in salary, for whatever reasons, failed to dampen this enthusiasm for his work and he records many years later: "After I had been one year in the service of the Village Missionary Society, I made a tour through the principal parts of the Midland Counties, and held meetings in most of the Churches in the General Baptist Connexion." His first visit was to Billesdon near Leicester and then to Hinckley, Coventry and Birmingham. He spent some time at Barton-in-the-Beans, and visited the Churches in the Vicinity. He records his meeting with Rev. Joseph Goadby at Ashby-de-la-Zouch and remarks on that pastor's ability to read from a Greek New Testament and translate as he read. He visited his birth-place, Melbourne, his first visit since leaving home, and held a series of revival meetings which excited great interest. His tour continued to Derby, Loughborough and surrounding villages and then on to Nottingham and Ilkeston. On his way back to Rutland he made his first recorded visit to Leicester.*

In 1831 the funds of the General Baptist Missionary Society failed and it found itself no longer able to support Thomas Cook as a paid agent. He was now forced to return to his trade as a wood-turner and cabinet-maker and set up in business at Barrowden. There was probably little even then in the way of remuneration and he made plans to move to Market Harborough, a more populated place. Nevertheless Barrowden provided another powerful influence on his life, because soon after he arrived he had met Marianne Mason who assisted in the running of the Baptist Sunday School. She was nearly two years older than he and had been born into a local farming family. Her mother had died when she was very young and, at just turned 21 when Thomas met her, she was well used to carrying the domestic responsibilities of her father and five brothers. The courtship lasted over four years before Thomas Cook, who had moved to Market Harborough in November, 1832, married her at Barrowden on March 2nd, 1833. Marianne was a remarkable woman and Thomas Cook proudly acknowledged her contribution to the business.**

---

*He recorded in a diary for 1829 that he had travelled 2692 miles in that year, 2106 of them on foot!

**A shrewd glimpse of Mrs. Thomas Cook is provided by Albert Bishop, mentioned above. In his letter to Thomas Budge he adds, 'I remember Mrs. Cook as a smallish very dapper lady who gave one the impression that she was all there - indeed my mother and father always considered that she had an even better business brain than her husband.

Thomas had signed the Pledge of Temperance on New Year's Day, 1833, just before he married, and Marianne had followed him in the Spring. Temperance and travel are not immediate associations but in their case the connection was to prove crucial.

The background to their new-found interest in temperance was the increased consumption of cheap home-produced gin. Behind this increase was legislation which had encouraged the distillation of spirits in Britain to counteract the imports of foreign brandy. The Government under the Duke of Wellington was greatly concerned at this increase. Their remedy was the passage of the Beerhouse Act of 1830. Mistakenly, they believed that if they encouraged the sale of "malt liquour" the consumption of spirits would decline. The effect was more gin-palaces and to the dismay of the Government, consumption increased by over thirty per cent. Despite further government action drunkenness persisted and eventually gave rise to a popular reaction which became the great Temperance Movement and Band of Hope so much associated with the later Victorian era.

In November, 1832 the Market Harborough Baptists, finding themselves without a minister, invited Rev. Francis Beardsall from Loughborough to preach at divine service. He was keenly interested in the Temperance Movement and was approached by the British and Foreign Temperance Society to becoming their agent for the area. The Baptist Church agreed as long as it did not detract from his pastoral duties.*

Thomas Cook himself, was not prepared to move any further than simple temperance and in fact still kept a quantity of beer and home-produced wine in his house and this is how the situation would have remained had it not been for the visit to Market Harborough of one John Hockings who rejoiced under the soubriquet of "The Birmingham Blacksmith". He came in the first week of December, 1836 and delivered a teetotal lecture in the Town Hall. His advocacy of the cause must have been very powerful for only a few hours later Thomas Cook and six others met in the parlour of a local businessman, Mr. W. Symington,** and enrolled themselves in a

---

*On December 16th, 1832 Thomas Cook was proposed for membership of the Church at Market Harborough and it was through Francis Beardsall that he and Mrs. Cook became involved with the Temperance Movement.

** Mr. Symington, (of the family that became famous for soups and ladies' corsets) was elected Chairman and Thomas Cook was elected Secretary.

Teetotal Society.

All this time the wood-turning and cabinet-making business was prospering. Employees presented a problem to Thomas Cook's teetotalism because they expected beer to be provided as part of their renumeration. This may explain Thomas Cook's initial reluctance, to move towards total abstinence and even after he had signed that pledge he still felt obliged to provide beer at his table for his workmen. The early teetotallers of Market Harborough found themselves a persecuted minority and Thomas Cook liked to tell of the difficulties. "Harborough", he wrote, "ranked in the estimation of the public as one of the most discordant and riotous of all anti-teetotal populations ... my house in Adam and Eve Street was violently assailed, and brick bats came flying through the window to the imminent danger of Mrs. Cook and myself. On one occasion a horse's leg bone, taken from a cart-loan of bones standing in the narrow street leading from the Market Place to Adam and Eve Street, was thrown at me with such violence that, striking me at the back of the neck, I was felled to the ground, and it is strange how I got up and gave chase to my assailant. But I did, and overtaking him identified him at the entrance to the Talbot Hotel yard. This case, like many others, was brought before the Magistrates, and convictions were obtained and heavy fines inflicted ... " This fine and others were probably paid by a notorious drinking club in the town known as "The Tenth". The house that was once occupied by Thomas Cook and his family in Market Harborough still stands, but is now used as a workshop and can be reached by means of an alleyway leading from Adam and Eve Street into Quaker Yard.

One of the great secular interests of non-conformists in the early nineteenth century was the Adult School Movement. The Baptist Church at Market Harborough ran such a school for its members, and Thomas Cook became superintendent very soon after he moved to town. Indeed by the summer of 1837 both Thomas and Marianne Cook could look back on their four years in Market Harborough with some satisfaction. Their business appeared to be sound and they had seen their interests meet with some success. They had one son, (another had died in infancy in 1835), and they were undoubtedly established members of their small Leicestershire community. Yet in 1837 a serious rift was developing in their relations with their Church. The Church Minute Book for August 24th records: "That in Mr. C's transaction with Mr. Knowles * we think he acted totally unbecoming as a tradesman and a Christian professor. That we are sorry to be compelled to believe on unquestionable evidence that he has been disgracefully inattentive to his word. That he be furnished with a copy of these resolutions, that J. Buckley. ** and Wm. Bennett shall visit him and endeavour to bring him to proper state of mind, and that he be suspended from the privileges of the Church till the next regular church meeting, when the matter shall again be considered, and if possible decided upon".

On October 5th, 1837 the regular meeting of the Church took place and Thomas Cook's case was the first item on the agenda, and he was summoned to appear on October 8th. At that meeting he was excluded from the Church despite expressions of penitence. But the affair rumbled on and after further meetings and what must have been prolonged agony, he was received back into the Church in February 1838. Unfortunately irreparable damage seems to have been done to relationships and a study of the available records from then until Thomas Cook's departure for Leicester in November, 1841 reveals very few references to him. Perhaps this rift encouraged him to devote more of his time and energies to the cause of abstinence with very important results.

---

*The Mr. Knowles referred to does not appear to have been a member of the Baptist Church for his name does not occur in any of the records of the period other than in the entry for August 24th, 1837. From the context of the entry it would seem that the matter causing the Church such great concern could have been a business affair entered into between Thomas Cook and Mr. Knowles.

** The J. Buckley referred to was most likely John Buckley who took over the ministry after the sudden death of James Thompson and that would indicate, by means of a pastoral visit, that the Church was very perturbed at whatever had happened. Over one month elapsed before we hear of further details.

II
THE RAILWAYS COME TO LEICESTER

"To Mr. Thomas Cook belongs the honour of being the first person to hire a special train at his own risk, sell railway tickets to the public, and personally travel with the train to look after the comfort of his passengers".

Clement E. Stretton.

In 1838 Thomas Cook was in his thirtieth year and although it was less than one hundred miles away, he had never been to London. In the Midlands the railway had, in fact, arrived earlier than in the metropolis. The Leicester and Swannington Railway, built by Robert Stephenson, had opened in 1832 primarily to move coal from the Leicestershire collieries to Leicester in order to meet the competition from Derbyshire and Nottinghamshire coal which was being transported in great quantities on the Leicester Navigation Company's canal. The Leicestershire coal interest had been effectively shut out from its own market. Led by John Ellis, a landowner from Beaumont Leys, they soon came to realize the importance and potential of steam locomotion as an industrial facility but like most people at the time, with the exception of George Stephenson, they did not envisage a national network of railways for the carriage of passengers. The Leicester and Swannington line when built did, however, possess a passenger carriage as well as coal trucks.

The first run took place on July 17th, 1832, with the train being driven by the great George Stephenson himself. It is reported that on this maiden run the engine chimney hit the roof in the middle of Glenfield Tunnel and it was forced to come to a halt on leaving the tunnel to allow its four hundred or so passengers, to wash off the soot and grime in a nearby stream! The new line was an immediate success and helped to recapture the Leicester market for the local colliery owners. Three empty wagon trains left Leicester West Bridge Station every day, excepting Sundays, at 8 a.m., 1 p.m. and 4.30 p.m. returning laden with coal. To this train a passenger carriage of the open "tub" variety was attached and passenger fares charged were a penny farthing per mile. Very soon it was apparent that a "one class" line for passengers was not sufficient and a first class carriage was built. It consisted of three compartments and the fare for travelling in this sumptuous style was doubled to twopence halfpenny per mile 1p. This line also had the distinction of being the first on which a "steam trumpet" or whistle was used. It was designed by a musical instrument maker of King Street, Leicester.

It was on this line that Thomas Cook made his first every journey by steam railway. He refers to this event in an article he contributed to a London publication called *Leisure Hour* in 1878 where he says, "I believe that the Midland Counties Railway from Derby to Rugby via Leicester was opened in 1840. At that time I knew but little of railways, having only travelled over the Leicester to Long Lane, a terminus near to the Leicestershire collieries". He gives us no indication of the precise date of his journey or why he made it. It could have been part of a tortuous journey to Derbyshire from Market Harborough to visit his mother. W. Fraser Rae, writing in 1891, records such a journey made by Thomas Cook's son, John Mason Cook, when the boy was six years old. That would put the date at 1840 and the account relates how it took four days of travel to arrive at Melbourne in Derbyshire. The portion covered by rail was on the third day. Although there is no mention of John Mason Cook's being accompanied by his father it is highly unlikely that a child of such tender years would have undertaken such a journey alone and more than likely Thomas travelled with his son.

Local reaction to railways resulted in the passage of the Midland Counties Bill and that passage was fraught with difficulties. Nevertheless an act creating a railway linking Rugby to Leicester, Derby and Nottingham received the Royal Assent on June 21st 1836. Work commenced and the first portion of the line, Derby to Nottingham, was opened to the public on June 4th, 1839. The second portion, from Trent Junction to Leicester, was opened on May 5th, 1840 quickly followed by the third part, Leicester to Rugby, on July lst, 1840. A handsome station was opened at Leicester, virtually on the site of the present London Road Station. It faced onto Campbell Street and was a two storey building with a fine portico. Cross-over and loop-lines catered for both up and down traffic from one platform and Leicester was now part of a network of railways extending from Yorkshire to London.

The name of Thomas Cook will forever be associated with early railway excursions yet he did not invent them nor, to do him justice, did he ever claim to have done so, but he did go so far as to claim that his special train on July 5th, 1841 "was the first publicly advertised excursion known in the country". He apparently believed that all of the excursions prior to his own were exclusively for members of organized clubs, societies or Sunday Schools and were consequently not publicly advertised. Thomas Cook was certainly aware of this fact as he wrote in the *Leisure Hour* article, "I had read of an interchange of visits between the Leicester and Nottingham Mechanics' Institutes". These reciprocal visits were to industrial exhibitions in the two towns. Certainly the Midland Counties Railway saw advantages in running excursions between these two cities.

But in 1840 Thomas Cook was not much interested in trains: he was however deeply involved with the Association's Tract Depository from which members of the various Temperance societies could purchase tracts, medals, ribbons and other insignia for use in their work. It was advertised as being in Adam and Eve Street, Market Harborough, and therefore would be more than likely kept on Thomas Cook's own premises. *The Temperance Messenger and Tract Magazine* which began life in February 1840 was described as "an organ of communication for the South Midlands Temperance Association".* His involvment in this work was most probably a direct result of the earlier connection with Joseph Winks, who did very much the same for the General Baptist Church. Thomas Cook had learned from him the value of the printed word and its dissemination. The Depository and co-editorship of *The Messenger* took up a great deal of Thomas Cook's time, though he was still engaged in the business of wood-turning. By early 1841 it is probable that Thomas Cook had finally given up wood-turning altogether and concentrated on his temperance work. Financially, it must have been very difficult for the Cook's to have made ends meet in their last years at Market Harborough. They had one son and Mrs. Cook had begun to take in temperance guests at their home in Adam and Eve Street, though she did this without enthusiasm.**

Those were precarious days for temperance organizations and

---

*The only copies which seem to have survived are those for 1840 and 1841 which are now part of the James Turner Collection of Goldsmith's Library in the University of London.

**This was perhaps the real beginning of the Cook's involvement with the travel trade and it prefigured the establishment of their temperance hotels some years later. Some commission was payable on his printed tracts but this did not amount to much.

there are many references to the pecuniary difficulties of the South Midlands Temperance Association. It employed agents but usually on a short term basis when funds were available and its existence was hand-to-mouth. Thomas Cook kept the Tract Depository going with considerable difficulty and eventually in 1841 took it over personally as a separate entity from the Association. With sole responsibility for the Tract Depository growing large on his horizon was the Quarterly Delegates' Meeting scheduled for July 5th. 1841. It was to be held at Loughborough and was too be, according to *The Messenger* of that month, "a Grand Demonstration of Rechabites and Teetotalers" (sic). As Thomas Cook walked the fifteen miles from Market Harborough to Leicester for a meeting in Humberstone Gate, he had an idea. Many years later in the *Leisure Hour* article of 1878 he described what happened on that fateful day.

> "From my residence at Market Harborough I walked to Leicester (15 miles) to attend that meeting. About midway between Harborough and Leicester - my mind's eye has often reverted to that spot - a thought flashed through my brain, - what a glorious thing it would be if the newly-developed powers of railways and locomotion could be made subservient to the promotion of temperance! That thought grew upon me as I travelled over the last six or eight miles. I carried it up to the platform, and strong in the confidence of the sympathy of the chairman, I broached the idea of engaging a special train to carry the friends of temperance from Leicester to Loughborough and back, to attend a quarterly delegates' meeting appointed to be held there in two or three weeks following. The Chairman approved, the meeting roared with excitement, and early next day I proposed my grand scheme to John Fox Bell, the resident secretary of the Midland Counties Railway Company ..."

The exact spot where the sudden inspiration came to Thomas Cook can be precisely located even today. Some years later he wrote that it "was on the way to Leicester, just after passing the Kibworth Congregational Chapel and Parsonage" These buildings still exist on the busy A6 road, solid red-brick constructions with the parsonage abutting the main road, on the Leicester side of the twin villages of Kibworth Harcourt and Kibworth Beauchamp. John Fox

Bell is reported to have told Thomas Cook, "I know nothing of you or your association but you shall have the train". Generously, or perhaps wisely, he personally contributed to the preliminary expenses. Arrangements were then made for the running of the excursion train. Curiously, *The Messenger* carries no reference at all to these particular arrangements and no record is to be found there of the actual excursion. The Loughborough meeting of July 5th, 1841, is referred to and the opportunity for those attending to use the railway is underlined: "Loughborough is a very eligible place for such a gathering, being within half an hour's ride, per railway, of the three towns" (Nottingham, Derby and Leicester), but no mention at all of the forthcoming excursion, arrangements for which must have been at an advanced stage when the copy went to the printers. For a contemporary account we must go to *The Leicester Chronicle*. The newspaper covered the occasion under the headline *Loughborough Teetotal Demonstration*. The account records that exactly 485 persons travelled by "special train" at a fare of one shilling a head return and "that both at Leicester and Loughborough there were from two to three thousand spectators assembled to witness their departure and arrival; and that every bridge along the line was crowded to have a peep at the train in progress" But no mention of Thomas Cook.

It seems very likely that no-one had realized the significance of Thomas Cook's undertaking, which ensured the meetings success. The fact remains that, despite the ungracious omission by those around at the time to give him the credit, his idea turned out to be very successful and laid the foundations of his subsequent career and the entire travel industry. That was the really "glorious thing" about July 5th 1841.

III
THOMAS COOK MOVES TO LEICESTER

"Mr. C. has had the merit of entering into an enterprise, which has proved the means of affording pleasure and improvement to thousands of persons, who, but for that enterprise, would never have visited many interesting scenes and places, and improved their minds by acquiring much useful knowledge".

The Leicester Chronicle 1850

The Temperance Messenger and Tract Magazine issued on November 1st, 1841 refers to Thomas Cook as being "formerly of Market Harborough". He had in fact moved to Leicester in September and so began a connection with that town which was to remain unbroken until his death in 1892. His time in Market Harborough had not been an easy one and it is probable that the larger town of Leicester, with its new connection by rail to London, seemed a more attractive field of operations than the small community of Market Harborough.*

Nevertheless in 1840 life in Leicester was very grim for many of its citizens. Unemployment was rife and in February of that year it was reported that poor relief had to be paid out to a quarter of the population. Most Leicester workers were employed in the hosiery trade or boot and shoe industry and so were vulnerable to the chances and changes in those trades. It has sometimes been assumed that the boot and shoe manufacturing industry did not become established there until after 1861 following a strike of shoe operatives in Northampton in that year. It is perhaps a little surprising then to discover that Thomas Cook lists in his 1842 guide and directory no fewer that 93 Boot and Shoe Makers compared to 70 Hosiery Manufacturers and in the 1843 edition 138 Boot and Shoe Makers to 84 Hosiery Manufacturers.

The street in Leicester where Thomas Cook made his first home was part of the new development that had taken place since 1810. One, King Street was on the edge of what had previously been known as the South Fields in the days of the open field system. This land belonged to the Corporation of Leicester which up to 1835 had been a "closed Corporation", a self-perpetuating oligarchy not above

---

*In fact he published guides to Leicester in 1842, 1843 and 1849 which tell us much of the city during this period.

speculating in any direction for the personal benefit of its own members. In 1804 an Act of Parliament for the enclosure of the South Fields was obtained and within a few years the Corporation set about selling land for building purposes. King Street was one of the results of this sale and it was laid out between 1812 and 1815. Building continued for some years and the development along the street was the most elegant that could be found in Leicester at the time and, although much altered, some of that elegance can still be seen, particularly in the graceful Crescent (c.1825) and, on the opposite side of the road, Crescent Cottages (1836). Thomas Cook's own establishment at the Belvoir Street end of the road has completely disappeared to make way for a modern office block.

Little of modern Leicester would be familiar to Thomas Cook. The New Hall, now the Public Lending Library, was built 1831-2 and adjoining is the "Pork Pie Chapel", so named because of its peculiar shape, which was designed in 1845 by J.A. Hansom of the eponymous cab fame. In Belvoir Street adjacent to the corner site occupied by 1, King Street stands Phoenix House (1842). It was originally the office of Samuel Stone, Town Clerk and author of "Stone's Justices' Manual". Thomas Cook and Samuel Stone, both exemplars in their separate fields, were thus once in adjacent premises. New Walk was laid out in 1785. In the 1840's most of it would have traversed open country but there was some building developing at the end nearer the town. One of these establishments, advertised in Thomas Cook's 1843 Guide, was an early swimming pool. The reader is invited to share the benefits of "tepid bathing" in "pure spring water" which "was constantly flowing and changing at the rate of about 9,000 gallons per hour". Charges were 6d. (2.5p) for both the public swimming bath and shower bath and 1s. (5p) for the private swimming bath and "China baths". In his introduction to the guidebook Thomas Cook recommends "all those who have faith in the doctrine of Hydriatism, or Hydropathy, to visit the New Walk establishment". The proprietor was a Mr. J.P. Clarke. The most significant development in Leicester in the 1840's was undoubtedly its connection with the growing network of railways in the course of construction throughout the nation. This increased Leicester's importance more than anything else at that time and may well have been one of the reasons inducing Thomas Cook to take up residence in the town. Apparently it took some time for the Midland Counties Railway Company to smooth out its operational difficulties and in 1843 Thomas Cook would not publish the time-table in his guidebook "on account of the frequent alterations which take place" Despite these initial difficulties the railway made Leicester a more advantageous place to live and with the opening of the line to Peterborough in 1848 and the extension of the West Bridge line to Burton-on-Trent a year later, Leicester's central position was ready to be exploited even more. *The Leicester Chronicle* for June 20th, 1846 was of the opinion that "the railway laid the foundation of the manufacturing improvement of this town".

Temperance work was still Thomas Cook's chief interest in 1841, and on September 18th, of that year *The Leicester Chronicle* carried an advertisement which informed the public that *T. Cook* was in business as a *Bookseller and Stationer* at 2 (sic), King Street, Leicester. There is no indication as to how he raised capital to purchase his printing press and stock in trade. We know that he had taken over the Repository of the South Midlands Temperance Association and had been indirectly helped along the road by the more affluent members of the Association but he was now widening his concern to include "all kinds of Periodicals, Unstamped Newspapers and Books of every description". He also advertised "Printing and Bookbinding in every department executed to order". His early months must have been hard work but he quickly published *The Leicestershire Almanack and Directory for 1842*, and *The Cottage Garden Allotment Advocate* - which was a small periodical.*

On December 24th, 1842, an advertisement appeared in *The Leicester Chronicle* announcing that the 1843 Guide to Leicester was ready for sale. "Compiled, Printed and Published by T. Cook, Printer, Bookseller and Stationer, 1 King Street, Leicester". This is by far the most interesting of all his publications at that time. In carrying out a survey of all the religious denominations in the town he prefigured the Official Census of 1851 which was the first census to deal with the question of religion. He delivered a questionnaire to every practising minister of religion in Leicester, the last question of which proved to be dynamite. It read, "What is the gross annual amount of money contributed by your congregation to religious or charitable objects?"

---

*Thomas Cook was an active member of the Leicester Allotment Society and in 1842 appealed for a fund to obtain a store of potatoes for the members of the society to be able to buy at cost price coupling this with a strong attack on monopolies. This appeal flopped.

In the advertising section of this Leicester Directory he took a page for himself announcing that "he keeps a Registry Office for Servants, and hereby proposes to establish a New Office which may be of great utility if properly supported, viz: A Registry of Private Lodging and Boarding Houses". No guide would have been complete without listing hotels, inns and beer retailers under their proper classification but in the advertising section there are, surprisingly, two advertisements for the drink trade. He was also involved with the *Anti-Smoker* - a spirited publication which reflected Thomas Cook's robust approach to life. but it had no future with a circulation of 500 a month. The problem for Thomas Cook at this time of his life seems to have been a shortage of capital and he had as yet no real record of commercial success to attract investors. By December, 1843 the *Anti-Smoker* had reached the end of the road and no more issues were published.

During 1843 Thomas Cook and his family moved from King Street. *The Leicester Chronicle* of August 26th refers to him now as being "of Granby Street", within easy reach of the station, and on September 9th the same paper carried another advertisement from him. As well as running a "Cheap Printing Office" at 26 Granby Street, he solemnly announced that "Commercial Gentlemen, Visitors &c. are respectfully informed that T.C. has opened his Establishment as a Temperance Commercial Boarding House, where Refreshments may be had at any hour of the day, and good Sleeping Accommodation is provided. T.C. is the general Wholesale and Retail Agent for Dawsons" Celebrated Turkey Aroma, the best substitute for Coffee ever invented. Agent for the Temperance Provident Institution". It is interesting that his first commercial connection with travel, with which his name is now synonymous, came not as an excursion agent but as an hotelier.

. . .

The public demand for railway travel was fast outstripping the operating companies' ability to deliver. Thomas Cook himself travelled extensively in the interests of temperance but the early railways were routed primarily for the transport of goods. Few had thought that people would become so interested in travel. The wealthy and educated minority had made the "Grand Tour" part of their development but now the poor and uneducated majority were, surprisingly showing a similar interest in sampling the adventures afforded by travel. For the railways, handling inanimate goods in transit was very different from dealing with large numbers of people. The response to this challenge eventually brought into being the Thomas Cook who became recognised throughout the entire globe. But he had a slow, uncertain and faltering start and for a long time was not widely appreciated as any sort of expert in travel. He is not even mentioned in connection with the special train which ran from Leicester for the Annual Gathering of Midland Total Abstainers held at Derby on Whit-Tuesday, 1844, and which carried about 1,000 passengers but he is listed among the speakers at the event. In the early 1840's he was undoubtedly involved in several railway excursions but in the absence of any contemporary evidence we only have his own accounts of this period. In 1860 Thomas Cook looked back on his time as an excursionist beginning with the trip from Leicester to the meeting in Loughborough in 1841:-

> "The gathering so fully justified the expectations formed of it, that I proposed a series of similar meetings to be held alternately in the three principal Midland towns, Leicester, Nottingham and Derby, and special trains were arranged for the purpose of facilitating these gatherings of temperance friends. This was the "day of small things" in Excursion Trains, and for three or four years the work was one of enthusiastic philanthropy bring with it its own reward, for during that time I never dreamt of it as a source of pecuniary interest. My sphere of amateur operations was bounded by Rugby, Nottingham, Derby and Birmingham, betwixt which points many thousands were initiated into travelling habits, and a foundation was laid for extended operations."

Later, articles tell us how in 1843 he organised Sunday School outings from Leicester during race-week. He took 3,000 children to Derby out of temptation's way but had to leave 1,500 "little enthusiasts" behind. They went the second day and he claims that 5,000 teachers and scholars took part in these excursions. The next two years must have been very formative years in connection with Thomas Cook's subsequent career. His own personal travelling had commenced in a big way in the early months of 1844 on account of his new periodical. *The National Temperance Magazine.*

Few people could have travelled so much by rail at that time and his imagination would have seen the potential offered by rail transport. Building on his own visit to Scotland over Christmas and New Year 1844-5, he announced on January 13th, 1846 in *The National Temperance Magazine* that he had "already effected partial arrangements for a Special Train early in the summer, from Leicester to Glasgow and Edinburgh" and he hoped that "a thousand Midlanders" would accompany him on the projected trip. His logistical problems for such a venture were enormous and his courage is to be admired. As he knew from experience, travelling over the actual border between England and Scotland by rail was difficult at that time.* Newcastle-on-Tyne was the northerly limit of railways in England and there was not even a through line from Leicester. From Newcastle there were steamers plying to and from Leith and Thomas Cook opened up negotiations with their owners for the conveyance of his party. Thomas Cook's negotiation with the General Steam Navigation Co. which ran the steamers from the Tyne to Leith were difficult and protracted, involving his travelling over the route making such arrangements as he could. His thoroughness extended to making notes of every point of interest that could be seen on the journey and negotiating for the accommodation of the party in Newcastle. All this, however, came to nothing for, despite his offer of £250 as a guarantee, he could not come to terms with the shipowners and was forced to abandon the idea of routing via Newcastle. His own journey to Scotland had been by the western route and it was to this that he now turned his attention. It necessitated yet a further visit north before he was in a position to announce in *The National Temperance Magazine* for June, 1846, a "Grand Midsummer Excursion to Scotland" to commence on June 25th. *The Leicester Chronicle* carried the advertisement for the trip on June 13th which made it clear that Thomas Cook was entirely responsible for the arrangements on this occasion. Tickets were to be obtained from "T. Cook, Printer, Leicester" which was the boldest venture he had ever taken and he was exposed to great risk. In fact it was not a success and this and the closure of *The National Temperance Magazine,* caused by financial pressures, led to Thomas Cook being declared bankrupt.

---

*The Queen and Prince Albert had begun to take holidays there from 1842 culminating in the building of the neo-Gothic Balmoral in 1855. A tide of tourism was reaching the remoter parts where roads hardly existed.

The bankruptcy hearings took place in Nottingham on January 15th and February 12th, 1847. It appears that Thomas Cook was himself the petitioner in these proceedings which could indicate that he probably had been trying to protect himself by his act of bankruptcy in the preceding summer. In 1846 debtors could still be flung into prison but that did not apply to bankrupts unless they were criminally so. Few details have survived of the proceedings in Nottingham, simply a few scant references in the newspapers. He obviously recovered from this state of affairs and there is some suggestion that he came to some arrangement with his creditors for on March 19th *The Nottingham Mercury* stated that a "certificate" was granted to Thomas Cook without opposition and was at pains to point out that he had come into court on his own petition. By April 9th he appears to have been completely discharged. Not surprisingly perhaps, Thomas Cook never referred to the incident of his bankruptcy, but the experience, must have been highly chastening and brought his fortunes within a whisker of disaster. How he recovered , so quickly, remains a mystery but he did have some well-placed friends, not the least among them John Ellis, the Deputy Chairman of the Midland Railway at the time, who was soon to play a significant role in the development of Thomas Cook's travel business. Nothing can be stated for certain except that Thomas Cook must have felt more confident of his financial position by Christmas, 1846 to have applied for his own examination in the court of 1847.

Despite the traumas of bankruptcy , within a few months we discover him making "an energetic speech" in support of a petition to Parliament protesting against the use of grain in the distillation of liquour. He had other causes on his mind as well, as he recounted many years later in *Birthday Reminiscenses,* 1891. "During 1846 and 2847", he wrote, "I was intensely interested in the progress towards Free Trade; and in connection with the repeal of the Corn Laws I took a very active part in promoting interest and excitement among the people. I published a little paper entitled *The Cheap Bread Herald,* in which my main object was to accelerate the downfall of Protection. His zeal brought him into conflict with the authorities and he received a summons. He had, in fact, fallen foul of the Stamp Act. Papers and periodicals which did not carry items of general news were exempt from stamp duty, not abolished on newspapers until 1861. It appears that *The Cheap Bread Herald* had contained a reference to the French Revolution of 1848 and for some reason this was deemed to be general news causing Thomas Cook to receive his summons.

The travel activities of Thomas Cook in 1847 are somewhat obscure. In his article for *The Leisure Hour,* 1878, he gives us his own account of the period:

> "The year 1847 opened more auspiciously for Scotland, and I had that summer three large excursions, the railways from York and Berwick to Edinburgh being available. But the High Level Bridge over the Tyne, and the bridge that spans the Tweed at Berwick, existed then in imagination only. In the autumn of this year I followed the Queen and Prince Albert over the route which they made royal, by the Clyde, the Kyles of Bute, the Crinan Canal, and the Atlantic coast to Oban, from thence to Staffa and Iona, circumnavigating the island of Mull, and afterwards visiting Glencoe, Fort William and the Caledonian Canal to Inverness. The great Highland coach road between Inverness, Dunkeld, and Perth became a favourite route long ere the first sod of a railway was turned".

It is most unlikely that he would be entirely responsible for three major excursions in the same year that he was a declared bankrupt. In fact his name does not appear in *The Leicester Chronicle* in connection with a railway excursion in either 1847 or 1848. There is an announcement by the Midland Railway of a trip to Edinburgh from Leicester from August 23rd to 30th, 1847 followed by a very scant report of the event later but there is no mention of Thomas Cook nor is there a mention of another trip to Scotland that year. The advertisement does corroborate Thomas Cook's statement the passengers had to walk through Newcastle and Berwick because there were no railway bridges. It is also true that, according to Queen Victoria in her *Leaves from the Journal of our Life in the Highlands*, she first passed through the Crinan Canal on August 18th, 1847, just five days before the departure of the excursion from Leicester so it could have followed her. However, Thomas Cook's involvement in any railway excursions is not absolutely clear until 1849.

In the summer of 1848 a somewhat curious excursion was arranged by Thomas Cook. In August of that year "109 respectably attired, and apparently happy individuals, mostly ladies" visited his native town of Melbourne in a convoy of nine crowded horse-drawn carriages and called at the Abbey of St. Bernard near Whitwick, Leicestershire.* When they arrived they encountered a little difficulty in that the Abbey Guest Master refused to admit them claiming that "it was contrary to the designs of the establishment to make it a place of rendez-vous for pleasure parties". Apparently a party of about 30, also from Leicester, had visited the Abbey the day before and they had misbehaved themselves "by exhibitions of intemperance, insulting observations, and acts of wilful damage to the property". Not to be put off by this Thomas Cook and a deputation secured an interview with the Superior and convinced him that the company they represented were principally teetotallers and that they would not stay beyond one hour. This advocacy seemed to do the trick and the party was admitted - ladies, however, were not allowed to venture beyond the lodge! They arrived at Melbourne at 12.30 p.m. Where they were met by "a powerful brass band of eighteen performers" and most of the 3,000 inhabitants of the town, to greet them. They visited the gardens of Melbourne Hall, took tea in the National School and at 5.30 endured the inevitable meeting where speeches on temperance were delivered. The party finally journeyed home through Loughborough.

   This successful visit led to a similar coach trip to one of Leicestershire's principal noble seats, Belvoir Castle, the home of the Dukes of Rutland. On August 29th, 1848, Thomas Cook organised an excursion to the castle consisting of over 70 persons in six horse-drawn carriages. The journey of 27 miles took 5 hours. On arrival the travellers were escorted through the castle in parties of 25. A handbook was produced for this trip. It sold at 3d. and contained notes on the route together with descriptions of the villages around Belvoir. It also included in the section entitled *Hints for Visitors* an exhortation to be on good behaviour whilst visiting the castle! Two more similar excursions to Belvoir were organised in the weeks immediately following. Two of the three are fully reported in *The Leicester Chronicle*. All these reports are in direct contrast to the adverse comments endured by Thomas Cook as a result of his first Scottish trip in 1846. A letter from the Duke of Rutland is quoted in full indicating His Grace's pleasure at the successful

---

*This was a new foundation, 1835, and was the first Cistercian abbey to be built in England since the Reformation.

accomplishment of the trips.

In May he made his first connections with continental travel by offering concessionary tickets, not excursions at this stage, to both Paris and Brussels. All of this was a prelude to a very considerable development in his travel interests. In July he organised a very large excursion to Scotland, the arrangements for which were to become a pattern of his activities for years to come. Early in the morning of Tuesday, July 24th, special trains left Leicester, Lincoln and Birmingham to unite at Derby for the largest excursion to Scotland by that date. "Feeder" trains left London and Peterborough on the day before and the travellers had been accommodated at either Leicester or Derby. Passengers were picked up at intermediate stations and when the "arterial" train from Derby reached Normanton, Yorkshire, another section from Leeds and Bradford was attached. It then continued by way of the east coast route to Edinburgh. *The Leicester Chronicle* carried a report on July 28th, 1849 which detailed the arrangements and continued:

> "The weather, so far, (to Normanton) had proved favourable; but soon afterwards it began to rain, and long before York had been reached, it fell very heavy indeed. Nor was this all - inconvenient and unpropitious as it undoubtedly proved to open-carriage travellers, most of whom were not clothed for such an emergency - the atmosphere was so dense as entirely to preclude anything like a distinct view of the country. There being no cessation of rain when the train had reached Darlington, Mr. Cook (the manager of the trip, whose attention to the comfort of the passengers, it is only doing justice to say, deserved much praise) applied for covered carriages for those who had been unfortunate enough to become the occupants of the Midland open ones. The request was at once complied with by the York and North Midland Directors, who immediately ordered closed carriages to be provided, at Newcastle, on the arrival of the train at that place, which were in readiness accordingly."

The travellers inevitably became exhausted but were awakened when the couplings broke leaving a number of carriages behind in the darkness! They were finally rescued by another engine, reconnected and the party of about seven hundred excursionists steamed into Edinburgh at 2 a.m.: The report continues:

"The rain was still falling very heavily, but the cabs and omnibuses were in attendance to convey the tourists to the various places set apart for their accommodation...Edinburgh is a wonderful place...worth undertaking a journey even like yesterday's...The passage over the skeleton bridge at Berwick was a frightful thing to contemplate. Let the inhabitants of Leicester imagine a number of boards put together - temporarily of course - over which nearly sixty carriages are whirled over a broad river, at a height of 150 feet, and they will somewhat realise the 'fear and trembling' which those who ventured to look down into the 'vast deep' experienced, in making this hazardous passage over the Tweed. Mr. Cook announced on the Calton Hill, that on the return, the passengers were to walk over, an announcement which was received with satisfaction."

In 1849 Thomas Cook published his last guide to Leicester. In it he appears as "commercial boarding house, coffee and news room, printer and newsagent, agent for the Temperance Institution". However, by April, 1850, there was the significant addition "Excursion Agent" The advertisement contained some of his plans for the year. The Scottish trip was to be repeated and later in July this was to be extended to include Ireland with the headline, "A Thousand Miles by Rail and Eight Hundred by Steamboat for four pounds". In August there was another excursion to Dublin via Holyhead. Scarborough was fast becoming popular as a holiday destination for people from the Midlands and Thomas Cook ran two trips there, each of about a week's duration. in July and September. At the same time as the September trip was advertised a correspondent to *The Leicester Chronicle* signing himself as "An Observer", entered a plea for even cheaper fares to enable more people to savour the facilities at Scarborough. Typically, Thomas Cook rose to the challenge with an advertisement on October 5th headed "A Call Answered" and announcing that the directors of the railway company had accepted his proposals for an experimental trip to Scarborough at an incredibly cheap fare of 6s. return, about half Thomas Cook's normal charges which were in themselves about one sixth of the ordinary fare! It was to leave Leicester at 1.30 p.m. on

Saturday, October 12th, arriving at Scarborough after II p.m. *The Leicester Chronicle* of October 19th stated that it had "proved to be one of the pleasantest, as it was decidedly the cheapest, of the trips of the season". The return was on Monday, October 14th with an option (for 2s.) to remain another day.

In November, 1850, a touching tribute was paid to this indefatigable organiser of travel. An advertisement on November 2nd announced a "Grand Testimonial Trip" to Cambridge. Apparently a group of his passengers on an earlier Scottish trip had formed a committee to raise a subscription to honour Thomas Cook with a presentation on account of "his having for nine years zealously and satisfactorily served the public as a projector and manager of Cheap Excursions". Accordingly, at 10.15 a.m. on Wednesday, November 6th, a train left Leicester for Cambridge loaded with about 800 people who had come from as far afield as Birmingham, Sheffield, Derby and places in between, to honour Mr. Cook. In the evening at Cambridge there was a concert in the interval at which he was presented with a gold watch and chain, 'value about £25" and suitably inscribed: "Presented to Mr. Thomas Cook by subscription, in approval of his able arrangements of special trips. Leicester, November 6th, 1850". Characteristically, he wanted to make a long speech of thanks but this was prevented.

By 1850 he was becoming famous in the Midlands and if he felt a glow of satisfaction we can perhaps understand it. He had taken 15,246 passengers over 7,520 miles with fares £5,090. 9s. 9d. *The Leicester Chronicle*, which only four years before had upbraided Thomas Cook for his want of satisfactory arrangements on his first Scottish trip was fulsome in its appreciation of his enterprise. His life was at last finding a purpose as he rapidly recovered from his bankruptcy of 1846-7.

IV
THOMAS COOK GOES TO EUROPE

"My constant aim has been to render excursion and tourist travelling as cheap, as easy, as safe and as pleasant as circumstances would allow".

Three aspects of Thomas Cook's activities were combining to bring him increasing prosperity, a substantial boarding house, successful printing business and travel interests were gaining recognition.

In 1850 Thomas Cook, and the Prince Consort had little in common. The connection between them was John Ellis, M.P., Chairman of the Midland Railway Company, a leading citizen of Leicester. Ellis played a significant part in the success of the Great Exhibition and his role has hardly been recognised. He was also to play an important part in the development of Thomas Cook's enterprise.

John Ellis was a friend of Joseph Paxton, a fellow-director of the Midland Railway, and an important member of the Duke of Devonshire's household at Chatsworth in Derbyshire. Paxton, had designed and built the conservatory at Chatsworth, and confided to John Ellis that he had an idea for the building which was to house the Great Exhibition. Paxton was given nine days to produce plans and the result was the famous "Crystal Palace", a bold, imaginative and revolutionary design which had the merit of being removable from Hyde Park after the Exhibition thus meeting objections from those who cavilled at the destruction of London's most important open space. By autumn of 1850 'exhibition fever' was mounting. A Provident Association had been formed in Leicester whereby people could contribute 6d. a week towards the cost of visiting the Exhibition and hope was expressed that between five and six thousand people from Leicester would make the journey. Travel would inevitably have to be by rail, a fact which doubtless interested both John Ellis as well as Joseph Paxton. Ellis knew exactly where to turn for help in organising the necessary travel arrangements. They met Thomas Cook in Derby and finalised plans for excursions to the Great Exhibition.

On January 18th, 1851 *The Leicester Chronicle* invited the public to attend a meeting to be held in the New Hall on January 21st. Thomas Cook is referred to as "the authorised agent of the Midland

Railway" and he was expected to speak "on measures necessary to be adopted to secure the privileges offered by the Railway Company". At this meeting he outlined provisions and encouraged people to travel to London announcing that the Midland Railway was making an investment by ordering 100 new carriages and at least 40 new engines for the expected stampede to London. It is small wonder that Ellis and Paxton had virtually ordered Thomas Cook to forgo a projected visit to America to concentrate on the Great Exhibition. It was anticipated that 100,000 people would travel to London from the areas served by the Midland Railway, of which 60,000 would come from the district allotted to him. This last figure in the event turned out to be something of an understatement. A reduced fare had been provisionally agreed between himself and the Board of Directors of the Midland Railway. He also arranged preliminary plans for day trips for those who could not afford to stay in London. "It might be late before they returned home", he is reported to have declared. "but he believed that many would cheerfully come back the same night, even if they slept in the carriages." Accommodation would be needed for the visitors and existing hotels and boarding houses in London were expecting a bonanza. Thomas Cook had visited London in the winter of 1850-1 in order to encourage boarding house keepers to register their accommodation with him but the request met with a poor response as the proprietors were prepared to wait in an attempt to get higher prices. The Midland Railway had declined to become involved in providing accommodation so Thomas Cook ventured into this area entirely on his own account, taking leases on several properties in London. One of these was near Vauxhall Bridge*" each person to have a separate dormitory, boxed off by a partition 7' high of which he would have the key. In these partitions there was to be a good bedstead with a sacking bottom and with a hair mattress". There was to be both a doctor and a barber connected with this establishment. All this was available at ls. 3d. per night and was to include one further important provision: "Should parties get into that state where they could not look after themselves at night, there would be a policeman in attendance to take care of them that they should not annoy other people"! The premises near to Vauxhall Bridge were situated in what was known as Ranelagh Road, Pimlico and were in the ownership of Mr. Thomas Harison. They accommodated up to 1,000 persons, presumably male, and were called by Thomas Cook,

"The Ranelagh Club Mechanics' Home". He advertised it in the magazine he launched in conjunction with the Great Exhibition entitled, *Cook's Exhibition Herald and Excursion Advertiser*. This magazine, later renamed "**The Excursionist**" continued to be published by the firm until the outbreak of the Second World War.

Entry to the Great Exhibition in its early days was five shillings, which effectively ruled out attendance by the artisan classes of people. It is not surprising, therefore, to discover that the first special train from Leicester was very much undersubscribed. It ran on April 28th, just prior to the royal opening, which Thomas Cook attended, and carried only 150 passengers. It was not until May 26th that entrance was reduced to one shilling and then the public began to flock to London. Thomas Cook's moment was rapidly approaching but there were still a few hurdles to cross before his greatest undertaking to date was to be safely launched. Thomas Cook asked the employers to help: "It is now quite clear that unless considerable aid is rendered, thousands who had anticipated a trip to London will be disappointed". There is evidence that many of the original members of the Provident Association had been compelled to cash in their savings in order to survive. On July 1st Thomas Cook wrote to Prince Albert and the Commissioners of the Great Exhibition asking for cheaper admission to the Crystal Palace. There is no record of a reply. A trade depression in Leicester made it difficult to persuade people to travel. He argued that there should be a four day ticket instead of separate entrance fees for each day. He reveals some of the waspishness of earlier days: "The funds already realised are more than ample to cover all expenses of the Exhibition, and there is no need to tax the poor country visitor to create a fund for the purpose of providing a public drive, walk, or lounge, for the wealthy denizens of the West End". Arrangements between Thomas Cook and the Midland Railway were completed and on June 7th *The Leicester Chronicle* announced that special trains would run to London from Leicester every day, except Sunday, with reduced fares late in the season for the benefit of the poor.

. . .

There is no doubt that the summer of 1851 gave Thomas Cook nationwide recognition as an expert in organised travel, but his activities with the Temperance Society were paramount in 1852 when the foundation stone of the Temperance Hall was laid on June 2nd, by the President of the Leicester Temperance Society, Rev. J. Babbington. Thomas Cook, whose main task that day was to present a silver trowel to the President, is described as a Director of the Temperance Hall Company and "Corresponding Secretary of the Leicester Temperance Society". Nine special trains had been run to Leicester for the occasion. The opening of the Temperance Hall (the first building in Leicester to receove piped water), took place on September 21st, 1853, with the Mayor of Leicester presiding. Special trains had again been organised from many parts. There were many lengthy speeches and the Chairman of the Temperance Hall Company announced that the cost of the building totalled £8,000 and alluded to "Mr. T. Cook and Mr. T. Corah to whom the honour of the whole design was due". While the building of the Temperance Hall progressed, Thomas Cook decided to build his own hotel adjoining it. He employed the same architect, James Medland, and an advertisement inviting contractors to tender appeared in *The Leicester Chronicle* on June 5th, 1852. Immediately after the laying of the foundation stone of the Temperance Hall. The hotel was apparently completed and in use before the Hall, for on May 7th, 1853 Thomas Cook was advertising "The New Temperance Hotel, Granby Street". Later, on September 20th, 1853, he organised a Public Breakfast in the Temperance Hall "to celebrate the erection and opening of the New Temperance Hotel" for which tickets were available at 2s. each.

The Temperance Hall in Leicester has long since gone, having ended its life as a cinema, but the adjoining hotel building still stands with much of the original facade intact. It has been much altered internally to accommodate a camping shop on the ground floor with the rest of the building serving other commercial interests. It served as the Leicester home and business premises for Thomas Cook until his retirement in 1879.

That Thomas Cook was in a position to undertake the erection of a substantial building for his own use is the most powerful piece of evidence for his increasing prosperity following the successful year of the Great Exhibition. But during all this building and construction he did not neglect the development of the travel enterprise, which gradually became the means of his livelihood. Working from the solid foundations of his experience with the Great Exhibition, be began in 1852 with what he described as his "Annual Spring Trip to

Birmingham" on April 26th and advertised no less than twelve arrangements for tours during that year, some of which, notably to Ireland, seem to have been on an almost continuous basis throughout the entire season. He resumed his Scottish tours, ran a trip to the "Birmingham Great Onion Fair" on September 30th and culminated his activities with special trains to London for the lying-in-state and funeral of the Duke of Wellington in November.

In 1855 he was to embark on another significant development - tours abroad. He made two preliminary visits to France and Belgium to make arrangements and his first conducted excursion to Europe commenced on July 4th of that year. The occasion was an exhibition in Paris but his tours were to include other places including Germany. He entered into an arrangement with the Eastern Counties Railway Co. to take his party via Harwich and Antwerp, travelling through Brussels to Paris. Despite the difficulties he took a second party on August 16th and appears to have made things a little easier. "In the former trip", he tells us, "we had to keep re-booking the passengers at every stopping place but we have now provided a ticket which will take the tourist upwards of 1,000 miles without further trouble". The tour carried the option of an extension to Germany and about 30 people, headed by Thomas Cook himself, visited Aix-la-Chapelle, Cologne, where they sailed on the Rhine to Coblenz, Mayence, Frankfurt and Heidelberg.

Like any modern tour operator Thomas Cook gave advice to his clients on two familiar subjects - money and language. "Money", he wrote, "is about as difficult to disburse in Prussia as it is to procure in England....The greatest annoyance is caused by ...the changes in currency and the rubbish of Prussian coins. To breakfast of Francs and Centimes; dine from Thalers, Groschen and Pfennings (sic); and sup on a medley of paper, silver and copper which few can comfortably digest, and much less is sustained by the 'small change' of a hundredth part of 10d. (1 Franc), the twelfth part of the thirtieth part of 3s. 2d. and the sixtieth part of 1s. 8d.. But we are prepared to help our tourist through this perplexity by negociating (sic) for them as much as possible and paying in bulk". And words that will be familiar to many a modern tourist: "They need not trouble themselves about changing money before leaving England - it may be done with more advantage abroad".

In his first Cook's Tour abroad was a lady known simply as "Miss Matilda" and she was accompanied by her three sisters. On their return they wrote a glowing testimonial which Thomas Cook, proudly reprinted in his magazine:

> "We would venture anywhere with such a guide and guardian as Mr. Thomas Cook, for there was not one of his party but felt perfectly safe when under his care.

There were many similar testimonials but, despite this fulsome praise heaped upon him these early continental trips were not a financial success; the proposed third visit that year was cancelled and in the following 1856 season a further planned tour failed to materialise for lack of numbers. Thomas Cook later complained that many of his first tourists had not taken up the option of the trip to Germany, upon which, apparently, financial viability depended. He evidently was to become wary of continental adventures, at least for the immediate future. None took place in the following years and in 1860 he wrote "we have abandoned all thoughts of invading France on a Tourist Campaign".

The Scottish excursions were the staple diet of Thomas Cook's business in the 1850's apart from 1857 when, in addition, he took 25,000 visitors to the Manchester Art Treasures Exhibition. It was on this occasion that he introduced his "moonlight trips" where travel in both directions was through the night thus avoiding more than one day's loss of work for his clients. In 1858 he advertised no fewer than six tours of the Highlands most of which would be personally conducted by himself. Each tour carried an optional supplement for an extension to enable the traveller to see more of Scotland. Thomas Cook would spend two months of each season in Scotland "heralding and conducting Excursionists and Tourists". One of the places visited was the island of Iona, long famous for its religious connections. There the excursionists found a population severely deprived and depressed. Whether Thomas Cook was the initiator of the relief subscription it is impossible to say but he obviously played an important part. In *The Excursionist* of August 23rd, 1858, it is reported that "more than £50 has been contributed by excursionists to replenish their (the Ionians) Library and to stock them with Fishing Boats, Lines, Nets, etc.." Apparently two boats were purchased, one of which was named *Brotherly Love* and the other *Thomas Cook*. *The Daily Bulletin* of Glasgow reported that "to these islanders Mr. Cook and his friends may be more useful than many Dukes".

. . .

By now a regular pattern was emerging as his travel business was slowly becoming established. It was probably in 1854 that Thomas Cook finally gave up commercial printing. The move to his new hotel had opened up further regular means of income. All the evidence shows it to have been successful and the development of Scottish tours in each successive season may have convinced him of the viability of the enterprise. He could be freed from printing to concentrate on travel - an activity not approved by *The Times* which on October 8th 1861 ran a critical leading article on what it called "excursion mania". It did not mention Thomas Cook by name but the allusion to his activities is unmistakable. It maintained that railway excursions were:

> an "overridden hobby" with the majority spoiling it for the few "nor do they (the excursionists) spoil their own pleasure only", it stated, "but they are beginning now to spoil the pleasures of the regular traveller. Grounds are being shut up, houses locked up, to keep out the invading hosts" ...
>
> ... The Excursionist knows that he has bought Nature below market price, and that is an undoubtedly successful transaction ... We doubt, however, whether Nature submits with so much readiness to be sold by contract, and whether wholesale raptures would not, upon examination, be found to be damaged goods".

After the loss-making excursions to the Continent in 1855 it was to be six years before Thomas Cook ventured across the Channel again. In 1861, however, he took part in organising what he called "The Great International Excursion to Paris". Fares were to be very low, London to Paris return for £1, and about 1,600 people took advantage of the offer. It was not a financial success and Thomas Cook later complained that the pecuniary loss was caused by his having to expend so much on advertising.

1862 was the year of the International Exhibition at South Kensington on the site of the present museum complex. It was opened on May Ist and Thomas Cook was involved in the arrangements for the visitors and took a lease on several properties in the area. One of them, 23 Ovington Square, was for "a select class of visitors", Thomas Cook making his own home there for about six months during the Exhibition season. He also advertised a "New Home of 100 Rooms". This establishment which became called "The Exhibition Visitors Home" was on Fulham Road opposite Pelham Crescent. He invested £1,000 in furnishing this property and the house was run on "Temperance Principles" though a smoking-room, however, was provided. Not content with accommodation and transport arrangements alone, Thomas Cook took a stand at the Exhibition Bazaar which was run alongside the main Exhibition. He described his stand as a "Court for the Exhibition and Sale of Scottish Productions". These included "Tartans and other Choice Fabrics, Ornaments, Jewellery and Confections" (but presumably not whisky) and in addition there was "An Office for the Issue of Scottish Tourist Tickets - all by Commission". He had been prompted to make all these arrangements, he said, "from his long and familiar acquaintance with most parts of Scotland".

Whilst he was making arrangements for the visits to London the Rail Company announced that there would be no more excursion trains to Scotland for the rest of the season. There was some suggestion that Thomas Cook had been abusing the concessions and selling excursion tickets for ordinary trains. In all probability the Scottish railway companies felt that he had shown what could be done and they were determined to take over the traffic themselves. Not surprisingly he railed against the decision in the pages of *The Excursionist* for by 1862 Thomas Cook was largely dependent on organised travel for the livelihood of himself and his family and the Scottish excursions were a vital part of the enterprise so that removal was a severe blow. Although he was free to continue his excursions to other parts of Britain as before, this, together with the watered down Scottish arrangements, could hardly guarantee a worthwhile income. But he was resourceful and his six months stay in London in 1862 gave him much food for thought. He decided to establish a presence in the capital as well as maintaining his office and hotel in Leicester. From the late summer of 1862 he was to be found at 59 Great Russell Street in premises which he called "The British Museum Boarding House". No trace of the building remains for it was later replaced by a block of flats. His work as an excursion agent was subject to planning regulations and he had to be discreet about advertising his activities. The only allowable designation was his name plate on the front door which simply read "Thomas Cook" with no mention of any business activities carried out within.

1862 was a decisive year for him. Not only was there the first London office but there was also an almost unnoticed development. For the first time he experimented with an inclusive ticket offering accommodation and meals as well as travel - the first "package". Hitherto he had always decided against this arrangement on the grounds of the differing requirements of individual clients but for that Whitsuntide he offered trips from Leicester to London which included accommodation. "Should this plan prove mutually agreeable to the Railway Companies, the visitors and ourselves it may be extended to other tours". In addition he had to consider new directions and it became clear that such expansion could be found in Europe he therefore visited Paris to arrange a tour and this was followed by an announcement of a visit to Switzerland. That journey was conducted by Thomas Cook on June 26th, 1863. The party crossed the Channel from Newhaven to Dieppe, rested overnight in Paris and made an early start for Geneva next day passing through Dijon, Macon and Lyons. After Geneva there were many options. It appears that between 130 and 140 travellers left London, the majority being ladies travelling first class. Travelling with the party was a lady called Miss Jemima Morrell. She was a member of a group that called itself "The Junior United Alpine Club". What is more important is that she kept a diary of the trip and gives us a detailed picture of events as they unfolded. Given the travelling conditions in Switzerland at the time the tour must have been a strenuous exercise. Thomas Cook is described by her as being of "Excursion fame" and it seems that he travelled onwards with them as far as Mont Blanc, Chamonix and thence to Martigny. There he left them to return to deal with other important tourist matters, "rather sadly" as Miss Jemima records. Only 62 persons of the total party actually travelled with Thomas Cook into Switzerland itself, since the remainder prefered to stay in France, rejoining the contingent for Switzerland on their return. The party continued onwards using various means of travel such as rail, diligence, on foot or by mule and made their way through Interlaken, Grindelwald and Lucerne where they could go by rail to Neuchatel and finally back to Paris en route for England. Thomas Cook was by no means exaggerating when he had referred to Switzerland as being a place for "enterprising and vigorous tourists". Few railways existed then in the country and the passes through the mountains must have been extremely difficult, if not downright scaring, even in summer.

Thomas Cook records an incident en route which gives some indication of how the nineteenth century excursionist had to manage.

"I had written to the proprietor of the Station Refreshment Rooms at Dijon", he wrote, "and telegraphed from Tonnere for dinner for 50 if he thought we had time to eat it. The timetable only showed 10 minutes, but on our arrival tables were set and a dinner good enough for the Emperor of the French was got ready, and was served with such rapidity that at least 25 got a capital meal in the short time the train stayed....There was no grumbling because the whole of the fifty did not dine, but the proprietor most courteously expressed his obligation, and ran after us as the train was starting, with three baskets of fine cherries".

Further trips to Switzerland and another to Paris were planned. In addition, he produced for the first time his Circular Tickets which were valid daily from London to Switzerland. These he printed in English and French and they enabled travellers to tour Switzerland independently. As he said at the time: "My constant aim has been to render excursion and tourist travelling as cheap, as easy, as safe and as pleasant as circumstances would allow".

The next barrier was the Alps and in October 1863 he left London for his first visit to the new Kingdom of Italy travelling via Paris and Geneva and Mont Cenis. He then took an extensive tour of northern Italy, travelling from Susa to Turin by rail and from there to Milan, Piacenza, Parma, Modena, Bologna, Porretta, Pistoia, Florence, Pisa and Leghorn, then to Genoa and from there spent two days travelling by diligence to Nice where he took the train through Cannes, Toulon, Marseilles and finally back to Paris, returning thence to England. In all he had made a round trip of some 3,000 miles. His first Italian Tour commenced on July 11th, 1864 and passed from Switzerland, through the St. Gotthard Pass and then to Italy, where after a twelve day visit the party returned via the Mont Cenis Pass. The trip was an evident success.

The extension of continental tours brought problems in its wake. One of these was that of imitation. One such company who attempted to use Thomas Cook's name in his advertising traded under the title of "Forian & Co." According to Thomas Cook, the proprietor "occupied the disagreeable position of a military conscript expecting shortly to be called into the services of the army". He was quickly seen off! Further opposition came from the English living abroad who were unhappy with the tourists and their case was explained by Charles Lever - later Consul in Trieste. He placed an article in *Blackwood's Magazine* of February, 1865, entitled "Continental Excursionists". It was later taken up by the prestigious *Pall Mall Gazette* and received considerable attention. Excursionists were described as "devil's dust tourists (who) have spread over Europe injuring our credit and damaging our character. Their gross ignorance is the very smallest of their sins. It is their over-bearing insolence, their purse-strong insistence, their absurd pretension to be in a place abroad that they have never dreamed of aspiring to at home". Charles Lever, also spread malicious lies concerning Thomas Cook in particular and the latter hit back in the pages of *The Excursionist:* "He, a British Consul, to whom in case of difficulty or emergency I may possibly have to appeal for that protection which is my right, deliberately asserts that he has spread among the Italians of his acquaintance a report that I am engaged by the Government of this country to take gangs of convicts abroad, and by leaving three or four at each of the different cities I visit gradually distribute the sweepings of our prison-houses over Europe". The controversy raged, the invective increased, over several months. Lever dubbed Thomas Cook "that fussy little bald man whose name assuredly ought to be Barnum"! Travel to foreign parts had hitherto been the preserve of the few Englishmen who could afford the "Grand Tour". Thomas Cook was encouraging "pretension" in his clients by taking them abroad - a far cry from "moonlight" trips to Scarborough! Expatriates who quickly saw that their idyllic existence would not for much longer remain inviolate. They were determined to fight to hold on to what they considered to be their exclusive right and privilege. *The Pall Mall Gazette* commented with a somewhat disapproving air: "To such a traveller Mr. Cook's excursion system must be a godsend. It enables him, at the least possible expenditure of time and money, to give himself all the airs of an extensive traveller".

Undaunted, further trips to Switzerland and Italy were arranged and in Holy Week, 1866, he escorted a party of about fifty to Rome. From that visit we can glean something of the almost makeshift way in which he was operating. What followed indicates either that he did not make, or was not able to make, proper provision for hotel reservations ahead of the party. It appears that when they all arrived at Florence, where accommodation was readily available, thay were advised that if they continued to Rome for Holy Week itself they would find all the hotels full. Thomas Cook had contracted to take the party to Rome and was determined that this difficulty would be overcome. He received information by telegram that he could rent a palace belonging to a wealthy Roman banker, Prince Torlonia, for 10 days at a cost of £500. Accommodation was only needed for 8 days in Rome and he telegraphed an offer by return of £400 for the required 8 days. Back came the reply £500 for 10 days or no deal! He called a meeting of his travellers and after some discussion it was agreed that he would stand £300 of the cost from his own pocket and that the tourists would pay an extra £4 each to make up the remaining £200, and they all proceeded to Rome on the basis of the plan agreed at Florence.

The Palace was large and roomy, near St. Peter's, but contained few facilities. Arrangements were made with the manager of the nearby Hotel de Rome to provide equipment to set up a dining room, provide the meals and attendant staff. Thomas Cook put on the bravest face concerning the inconvenience saying that "those who travel in Italy must expect sometimes to have to sit on hard seats and place their feet on hard floors, and they will do well if they never fare worse than was our lot in Rome during the eight days of our occupation of the Palazza Torlonia". The accounts of the hotel transactions were published. They show that Thomas cook's expenditure on accommodation for the tour amounted to just over £853 including the £500 for the rent of the palace, paid for 10 days but occupied only for eight, and receipts of £847 including the £4 "surcharge" from each member of the party.

V
EXPANSION

Leicester would always remain home to Thomas Cook and his family but in May, 1865 it was announced that a third set of business premises at 98 Fleet Street, London, was to be added to the growing empire. The makeshift office in Great Russell Street under the management of Miss Muglestone but as the only London base had obviously proved inadequate.The newly acquired building was near to St. Brides Lane and consisted of offices and retail space with a commercial boarding house, on the upper floor. His son John was to look after the office and Thomas Cook himself was glad to be relieved of a lot of desk-work so that he was free to escort travellers, and in 1866 he left Liverpool in "The City of Boston" bound for New York. In all he was away from Britain for 11 weeks and toured 4,000 miles in the U.S.A. and Canada making what arrangements he could for a forthcoming conducted tour.

He was impressed with the American railroads and delighted in the fact that sleeping berths were provided - as yet unknown in Europe. He visited Hamilton and Toronto, saw the Niagara Falls, continued on to Detroit and then Chicago where he marvelled at a city of 196,900 inhabitants whereas in 1830 there had only been 70 people! In Cincinnati he saw the steamers on the Ohio River on their way from Nashville and Louisville. He spent 10 days in New York and visited Philadelphia, Baltimore and Washington DC. Nevertheless the first party to America was not by him for it was announced in *The Excursionist* that John Mason Cook would leave Liverpool with a party of tourists on April 25th, 1866. It was also announced that there were plans for tours *from* America *to* Britain.

. . .

The middle years of the nineteenth century were the golden age for industrial exhibitions and the dawn of 1867 was to see Thomas Cook making arrangements for visitors to attend the Paris Universal Exhibition to be held that year. He visited Paris looking for accommodation premises and was even bold enough to attempt to enlist the help of the Emperor Napoleon III but without success. Eventually he did find premises which could accommodate 100 "working class" people and which were situated at 15 Rue de la Faisanderie, Avenue de l'Imperatrice. He was to call this his Anglo-American Exhibition Hotel. Another set of premises at 3 Boulevard Haussman was to become his Spring Boarding House. He had five distinct apartments for the accommodation of persons of "superior class". He also opened an accommodation register for hotels in an office he set up in the London and New York Hotel in La Place du Havre.* His accommodation premises for the visitors were daunting. "We took from England", he wrote, "almost a ship load of furniture, bedding, etc.; and four out of five crates of Staffordshire fine China and earthenware by mistake got into the Exhibition". These items appear to have taken a fortnight to retrieve! As if these problems were not enough he was insistent on running his accommodation in accordance with his temperance principles. His one exception was to provide wines for his better class of client. Temperance hotels were unheard of in France and his Anglo American Exhibition Hotel which was (later extended by means of garden huts to accommodate 250) must have been an object of curiosity. The place was managed by Mrs. Cook and their daughter, Annie, who could speak French; and they encountered servant problems over the question of drink. For all its difficulties the 1867 Paris Exhibition provided another fillip for Thomas Cook's growing business. He calculated that he took 20,000 visitors to Paris and accommodated about half of them under his arrangements. Again, he had to deal with the problems of working with a Committee and 1868 saw quarrels with Mr. Hodgson Pratt, the Honorary Secretary of the Paris Exhibition Committee. Most of the differences concerned the question of advertising costs and who should bear them. It was also revealed that Thomas Cook did make some money from his Anglo American Hotel but lost heavily on the premises in Boulevard Haussman. The year 1868 saw the introduction of an important scheme to beat the vexed hotel problem by the invention of the Hotel Coupon exchangeable for accommodation and meals at several selected hotels in France,

---

*In 1861 he had failed to make proper forward provision for the accommodation of his own private party with the result that he and about eight others had been forced to wander the streets of Paris for about 3 hours "with carpet bags and other luggage" until they found available lodgings. Once installed and, as he admits, through a complete misunderstanding they had to pay over the odds for breakfast. Accommodation arrangements were proving a hard nut to crack.

Switzerland and Italy with which Thomas Cook had an arrangement. By this means travellers could purchase any number of coupons at 10 francs each and so pay for accommodation prior to departure. The scheme was an immediate success and by October, 1869 it was announced that 26,000 coupons had been sold. This was a major development akin to the later travellers' cheques and in its own way removed the need for tourists to carry huge sums of money, usually in good coins, en route.

Thomas Cook's next venture was to the Middle East. Few hotels existed there at the time and the prospect for Thomas Cook's intrepid travellers was tented encampments. On January 24th, 1869, the first party with Thomas Cook and two assistants left London for the 105 day tour of Palestine and Egypt, by way of Brindisi and then by boat to Alexandria. They travelled by steamer up the Nile to Thebes where the career of Thomas Cook was almost cut short. He decided to swim in the Nile and was quickly in difficulties:

> "Whilst bathing in shallows over the sands, I became instantaneously the sport of a rapid under-current, was carried beyond my depth, and the boatman had to reach out an oar to my rescue, whilst a group of Arabs on the shore called upon Allah to help me! - themselves, as I afterwards learnt, dreading to come to my rescue under the impression that a crocodile had seized me....This was my first and last attempt at bathing in the Nile".

Not all of the tourists in the party visited Egypt. There was also a shorter 70 day tour which only went as far as Palestine. The two groups were to meet at Jerusalem and when complete consisted of a total, including Thomas Cook and his two assistants, of 52 persons, out of whom 16 were ladies who must have been extremely adventurous to attempt such a tour at such a time. Whilst in Palestine they were conducted through the country by Dragomans* to look after all the necessary equipment for camping. Commenting on the visit, Thomas Cook wrote from Palestine:

> "It is a great consolation that at the present time there are no serious impediments to Palestine travel. The country is remarkably free from epidemics, and the tribes are at peace ... The lack of smooth roads and easy roads is the chief

difficulty. Sometimes travellers fall into the hands of haughty, imperious dragomans*, who lord over them with almost unbelievable hauteur; and as none can travel alone here, all have to submit to this disagreeable necessity....A tour is proposed, horses, mules, tents, provisions of all kinds are arranged, and the traveller is committed to the care and control of his dragoman for 20, 30, or 40 days, for which payment must be made, whatever happens to the tourist".

The two groups converged and encamped together just outside Jerusalem a few days before Easter and on the night of Good Friday, March 24th, disaster struck. They were robbed. Everyone was quite exhausted after a three day trek to the Dead Sea and three tents, including Thomas Cook's, were entered and all the baggage taken. The perils of travel in those days are well illustrated by the fact that Thomas Cook was carrying £450, an enormous sum in those days, in gold napoleons, all of which were taken. He was left with 30 gold sovereigns when the rifled baggage was eventually retrieved. The Turkish authorities first of all arrested the servants but Thomas Cook was certain that they were not the culprits and had them released. In fact the robbers turned out to be peasants. Much property was recovered but not all of Thomas Cook's money. The flocks and lands of the thieves were impounded and it looked as if the famous excursionist would be in possession of land in Bethlehem as recompense.**

These early Cook's Tourist of the Middle East undoubtedly possessed a strong spirit of adventure. They had to contend not only with robbers but with the storms which periodically blew down the

---

*Arab guide.

**In 1872 repercussions from the robbery in Jerusalem again arose. Thomas Cook had looked with some amused interest at the possibility of owning property in Bethlehem as recompense for the money which had still not been recovered. The thief was soon to be released from prison owing Thomas Cook the sum of £250, £100 of which was represented by the house and land in Bethlehem which was now made over. Thomas Cook, who obviously had no personal use of such a property, was anxious that it be used for Christian purposes and declared that he would hand it over to a Christian organisation if a subscription of £75 could be raised, which would be paid to him to make up some of his loss. He seemed to be having some difficulty with this as by the middle of 1872 he could only count on a total of £6.

tents as well as hard days in the saddle to see the sights they had come to visit. The group which took in Egypt travelled 7,600 miles in the 105 days of which 33 were spent travelling horse-back. As well as Egypt and the Nile they had seen the River Jordan, the Dead Sea and the Sea of Galilee with all the places in between including Jerusalem, Bethlehem and Damascus. They returned via Turkey, the Balkans, Venice, Switzerland and Paris to London. The "Grand Tour" had become a little less grand; the East a little less mysterious. Thomas Cook made a further visit to the Middle East later in the year when he was present at the opening of the Suez Canal in November, 1869.

In time Middle Eastern tours now became an established part of the itinerary of the firm of Thos. Cook and later the Nile steamers were taken over by the firm itself. By that time John Mason Cook was in complete control of operations, having forced his father to retire, and their organisation of transport on the Nile was so efficient that when, in 1885, the British Government ordered the abortive attempt to rescue General Gordon at Khartoum it could only turn to the firm of Thos. Cook & Son for the organisation of the required transport.

VI
NEW FRONTIERS

At the beginning of the 1870's there were three permanent offices in England - London, Leicester and Manchester - and agencies in Liverpool, Glasgow and Edinburgh. In continental Europe the firm was represented in Paris, Brussels and Cologne; in the Middle East it had agents in Alexandria, Cairo and Beirut. Thomas Cook was now in his early sixties and must have come to rely on his son more and more as the expansion continued. When John Mason Cook entered into a legal partnership agreement with his father the firm became known as Thos. and John M. Cook, later to be altered to Thos. Cook & Son - a title which remained in being for many years. Father and son were now joint proprietors of what had certainly grown to become a going concern with a high reputation.*

Continental travel was soon threatened by the outbreak of the Franco-Prussian War. Thomas Cook left for Switzerland in July 1870. On his return in August he addressed a letter to *The Times* assuring everybody that all was well. Describing himself as "agent of French, Swiss, Italian, Rhenish, Holland, Belgian and German (railway) companies" he says that his office in Fleet Street was besieged with personal and written enquiries as to the safety of travel on the Continent. He claimed "Switzerland was never more attractive to English visitors than it is at present, and although prices of provisions are enhanced, hotel charges with very few exceptions remain the same, and are likely to continue at about the present rate. In the absence of other peoples, it is natural to suppose that English and American visitors will be heartily welcomed by hotel proprietors and other traders. Some tourists may not have wholly agreed with his rosy picture. *The Times* also carried letters from English travellers who had been arrested in Paris on the suspician of

---

*In a debate in the House of Commons on the National Expenditure it was suggested by the M.P. for Brighton, Mr. White, that "Mr. Cook, the Excursionist" be permitted to organise the transport of troops within the United Kingdom as he, Mr. White, was sure that it would be done more cheaply and, incidentally, with greater comfort for the troops!

being Prussian spies! * Despite all the disruption caused by war, however, one of the travellers under the auspices of Thomas Cook at this time was Campbell Tait, Archbishop of Canterbury, who in late 1870 travelled across Europe to San Remo, Italy.

Expansion led to new premises being established in London and in April 1873 *The Excursionist*, carried on its title page for the first time the illustration of the new premises in Ludgate Circus, London. Thomas Cook wrote: "We have some time felt that our business was growing to such a magnitude, that we were not only justified but bound, to give our patrons and ourselves the best accommodation we could; therefore we watched our opportunity and secured what we say is the best corner in London for our purposes". The buildings were the first purpose-built headquarters of the travel firm (the Leicester office was built primarily as an hotel) and still stand today, although long since vacated by the firm. They served as business headquarters until well after the First World War. Thomas Cook arranged for a visit by the Knights Templars from the USA to England. Included in the party was a certain "Sir Knight" Edwin M. Jenkins. This gentleman, described as coming from Alleghany, was interested in working jointly with the Cook's to organize parties of tourists from America to Europe and in 1872 Thomas Cook announced that Mr. Jenkins "had entered heart and soul into our arrangements and is zealously working out the organisation of Parties for European and Eastern Tours". 15 April, 1873, "Thomas Cook, Son & Jenkins" was operating from 262 Broadway, New York.

■   ■   ■

Although it was to be a few years before he retired, Thomas Cook continued to travel and planned to circumnavigate the entire globe. This expedition proved a fitting climax to his long career of personally conducting tourists. He was approaching his 64th birthday

---

*It must have seemed necessary to go to considerable lengths to ensure the smoothest possible functioning of the continental traffic for in *The Excursionist* it is recorded that Thomas Cook sent his representative, Mr. Ripley, to Paris for interviews at the British Embassy, with the Prefect of Police, the Minister of War and the Commandant of the First Division of the Army in Paris "to all of whom we explained our tourist arrangements and from all received assurances of friendly assistance in case of need.

and he was never again to undertake such a long expedition. It is not clear what exactly induced him to contemplate a trip round the world, but in any event he announced in June, 1872, that the tour was to commence the following autumn. He debated for some time whether to include Australasia in the itinerary but finally decided against that, resolving to travel by way of Japan and China instead. The cost of the tour was fixed at a basic 270 guineas (£283. 50) with the inevitable options. He also decided to give each of his travellers who paid £30 deposit the names and addresses of all the others, "so that they may start together with mutual acquaintance, or, at least, mutual knowledge of their travelling companions". Perhaps as expected, such a large undertaking did not attract a great number of clients and not all completed the entire circumnavigation but the significance of the tour lies in the fact that it must have been the first time a round the world journey had ever been organised for a purely leisure activity.

During the tour* Thomas Cook wrote a series of articles for *The Times*, the first one from San Francisco, giving some information regarding his clientele:

> "My pioneering party is not large, eight today, maybe eleven when we sail hence tomorrow, but we represent, in pleasing harmony, England, Scotland, Russia, America and Greece". Later in the same article he described how they have sailed from Liverpool on board "The Oceanic" of the White Star Line, spent five days in New York and then travelled to Niagara, Detroit, Chicago, which was just recovering from a disastrous fire, Omaha and Salt Lake City where he was very impressed with the industrious nature of the Mormons. He recounts his encounter with North American Indians: "Prairie fires on all sides, antelopes, wolves and Indians kept us in a state of almost constant

---

*On this tour Thomas Cook never altered his watch, regarding that as too inconvenient and relying on geography to bring him back into line. In San Francisco he contemplated his first crossing of the International Date Line in picturesque style: "We have gone with the setting of the sun until my watch, which still adheres to the Old Country time, points to 5 a.m. tomorrow, it being here but 9 p.m..I expect somewhere in the Pacific to lose a day, and then our next land will be that of the rising sun, travelling in the course of which we will regain the losses of his decline in the west".

excitement. The Sioux tribe were evidently on the move to southern quarters, as they were mounted, in great force, on both sides of the line. They were supposed to be 500 at least, all mounted on very fine horses, gaudily dressed, and armed to the teeth. Had they been hostile they might have troubled us by closing in their extended lines; but they gave evidence of friendship by cheers and actions, waving of caps and other signs of mirth."

Japan impressed him so much when they called at Yokohama that he bought a rickshaw to be shipped to England. This piece of oriental transport was eventually presented by Thomas Cook to The Towers, a hospital for the mentally handicapped in Leicester. The visit to Shanghai lasted 24 hours on account of the filth and pestering beggars and they took a coaster to Hong Kong where they boarded *The Mirzapore* en route for Singapore. On December 21st they were in Penang where Thomas Cook spent £5. 2s. on a telegram of Christmas greetings to England. Christmas Day itself was spent on board *The Mirzapore* off Sri Lanka (Ceylon in 1872) in a temperature of over 80 degrees Fahrenheit and in the New Year of 1873 the party arrived in India. A Saloon carriage, complete with "sleeping berths, baths and closets" was put at their disposal for three weeks and arrangements were made to attach it to any regular train available. In this way 2,300 miles were covered in India. Thomas Cook was looking for hotels for future travel arrangements remarking that bedding would be required in some "where it is only customary to provide bedstead, mattress, one sheet and perhaps one hard pillow".

At Agra he spoke to a temperance meeting of 500 British soldiers, "a more enthusiastic meeting on temperance I never attended". He railed against the evils of drink and vice and was quick to see the effect on the local population: "Young men released from the restraints of home are dying of drink rot; morals are sapped and undermined, the Church loses its members, and the standing and withering question of the heathen, when pressed and beaten in argument, is, to point to the drunken sailors, soldiers and civilians. Is it like them you wish to make us?"

He posted that particular despatch to *The Times* in London from Suez at about the beginning of March, 1873. In Egypt he had to leave his party to make their own way. Apparently the tourist season in the Middle East was proving to be the busiest to date and Thomas Cook had to concentrate on the needs of about 75 travellers who were depending on him to make arrangements for tours around the area. The firm of Thos. Cook & Son were now acting as agents for the Khedive of Egypt and his government in arranging tours by the Nile steamers for visiting the archaeological sites and in the spring of 1873 they found that the hotels in Cairo were almost full with visitors wishing to sample the delights of Egypt. Leaving Cairo he arrived in Jaffa on March 9th and there found much to complain about. The steamboats that plied up and down the coast from Egypt had obviously not adapted their time-tables for the convenience of visitors. Services were offered one way for three days followed by a gap of about ten days with no sailings. Thomas Cook thought this quite unacceptable because it left travellers "with no means of getting from Alexandria, Port Said, etc. to Jaffa, Beyrout or Smyrna. The passengers coming this way are thus thrown together in confused heaps, while hundreds have this year given up all attempt to get from Egypt to the Promised Land". He had, it seems, pulled strings for his own party but had a guilty feeling about it; "I have got my largest party through thus far by long precautionary arrangements, but it is not pleasant to fill berths and state-rooms of steamers to the exclusion of others". The tourist boom was definitely under way and not for the last time locally provided services were proving inadequate.

By April 12th he had been away from home for nearly eight months and possibly the strain of being responsible for tourist arrangements without a break for so long was telling on him. He was in Constantinople on his way home. There are signs that he was feeling somewhat jaded as he writes very disparagingly of that city and its hotel accommodation, or lack of it: "Round the world I have not found a larger place so wretchedly provided with hotels as Constantinople; and I shall be glad when, on the Sea of Marmora (sic) 'homeward bound' we turn our backs on the Golden Horn". During his absence abroad, he had promised his wife, Marianne, that he would write her a letter every Sunday. Those which survive are mostly devoid of business discussions and concentrate on family matters of mutual concern. In what appears to be the first one from his world tour, written crossing the Atlantic on October 6th, 1872, he refers to having been hampered by sea-sickness but had managed to take part in the on-board entertainment where he was asked "to give some particulars of my work and my present object in coming to America. On October 20th he was writing from Chicago where the newspapers had apparently reported his arrival. He had not forgotten his devotion to the cause of temperance, and noted with approval that "the Americans do not provide drinks on the table, and only the English and Scotch people call for them ... Iced water is the Beverage of the Tables". The Sunday afternoon of November 3rd, 1872 saw him on board *The Colorado* somewhere in the Pacific. He was not attended by a personal servant although some of his party had their servants with them and arrangements had to be made to re-accommodate several man-servants away from the 500 mostly Chinese and Japanese steerage passengers. A somewhat curious picture of his own arrangements is revealed in his letter of that day to "My Very own Marianne, I intended to enclose you, as a curiosity, my Salt Lake washing bill but don't know what has become of it. The items were three undershirts, two flannel so called 'large articles'; twenty five collars, fronts cuffs and handkerchiefs - all for the sum of $4.30....That was my only 'wash up' since I left home and I don't think I will wash again until we reach British India". Considering that he was at Salt Lake City in late October and not expecting to arrive in India until the New Year it is an interesting revelation!

In what must have been one of his last letters home on that tour we see the first evidence of the impending family storm that was soon to engulf them. There is in the letter a hint of the gap that was opening up between father and son. The letter was dated March 24th, 1873, on board *The Mars* - leaving Palestine:

> "I have received a painful letter from him (John) in reply to one I wrote on the Red Sea. But I am not going to distress myself. I know my heart is right towards him, and towards yourself, and my dear girl also, and I shall not be moved from the path of Duty to either division of my family. He does not like my mixing Missions with business: but he cannot deprive me of the pleasure I have had in the combination; it has sweetened my journey and I hope improved my heart without prejudice to the mercenary object of the tour. I shall neither be expelled from office nor stifled in my spirit's utterance, and I have told him so very plainly."*

---

*Simply making money was never enough for Thomas and he always found time to mix business with the other serious pursuits of his life. This inevitable led to clashes with his single-minded son who objected to the use of business time, and money, for his father's pet causes to the detriment, so he believed, of the firm of Thos. Cook & Son.

Before the final parting of the ways between father and son, however, there was to be one very important and far-reaching innovation with the introduction of the travellers' cheque or "Circular Note" as it was first called. This innovation was heralded in the American edition of *The Excursionist* for June, 1874. Thomas had already seen at first-hand the dangers of carrying gold when he was robbed in Jerusalem and the Hotel Coupon system he invented proved to be a step on the way to providing safer arrangements for carrying funds whilst on tour. The method which has now become universal was first used in America and arose out of requests from clients of Cook, Son & Jenkins for the firm to hold funds which could then be drawn by the client in local currencies as required. At first they refused, pleading that they had not the machinery to operate such a system, but finally devised a scheme whereby cheques were issued from the London headquarters.

Father and son were continuing to clash with one another and further evidence of their different approach is provided by the Cook v Jenkins saga. The Cook's had virtually set Jenkins up in business in New York. They had put $5,000 into the firm of Cook, Son & Jenkins and advanced Jenkins a further $5,000 to represent his own contribution. He was to receive half the profits and be allowed to draw up to $2,500 p.a. against his half. From his share he was to pay back, by instalments, the money he owed his partners. After a few years Jenkins broke the agreement, overdrew, and finally decamped in 1878 still owing them over £3,000. John Mason Cook proceeded with prosecution to recover the debt but claimed in a letter to his New York lawyers that his father would not support him and that Thomas even wished to re-instate Jenkins with the power to use the Cook name in business. Jenkins in turn sued John Mason Cook for libel and claimed $50,000 damages. The case dragged on until 1883. Jenkins became seriously ill and John was advised to call of the case, but he refused unless judgement was in his favour. Judgement was given in favour of Jenkins but with damages fixed at a derisory 6 cents, a clear reflection on the character of Edwin M. Jenkins who Thomas Cook had so obviously misjudged. Jenkins died in December, 1883, and presumably the Cook's never saw their £3,000. The Jenkins case aggravated the tension that existed between father and son. John Mason Cook had always had reservations about working with his father.

When the row finally broke it divided the family. John had married and had children of his own. Ranged against him, apparently, were his father, mother and sister, Annie. Matters came to such a pitch that in November 1877, John issued a statement and went to the lengths of lodging it with a solicitor. From it we can glean something of the issued which divided them. In his statement John accuses his mother and sister, but curiously not his father, of making scurrilous remarks about him. He accused them of falsely stating: That his mother and sister had received no benefit from the business since he had been connected with it: That he (John) had repeatedly referred to the large amount lost by his father through his old business (corn and hay) in Leicester and that he had cleared the mortgage on the hotel in Great Russell Street with his father's money: That he did not understand how to treat a partner: That he took the monies from the firm to build the Ludgate Circus headquarters without his father's consent and that he had not paid any interest on the monies so used: That he was killing his father by the criticisms he made of him: That he was now treating the family as he and his wife had treated "poor dear Grandfather who is gone". This point must refer to earlier family troubles but the fact remains that John was definitely more successful at making money that his father and this may well have rankled. John Mason Cook claimed that he had turned the excursion business round in 1865 and that as a result the mortgage of £1,100 on the Great Russell Street hotel had been paid. He also claimed that when his father came to hear about the repayment he "flew into a passion and declared that I had either robbed him or somebody else to enable the money to be paid". His achievement in clearing the mortgage, he further asserted, enabled his mother and sister to live in the property rent-free. As a counter-blast he declared that his mother had taken £2,000 for her private account from the Paris hotel funds in 1867 whereas it should have been returned to the excursion business which had financed the setting up of the hotel in the first place. He also averred that Thomas had proposed a partnership agreement with him and that he, John, had first objected: "I reminded him that we never worked well together, and that our ideas of business were so opposite that I did not believe we ever could". He also complained that his father "spent a great portion of his time (and a portion of our assistants') ...devoted to innumerable private correspondents and to private matters quite outside our business". The root of that trouble may well have been that Thomas had become so used to doing as he pleased with the firm and its resources that he saw no reason to change his ways when his son became a partner.

It must have been clear to the whole family at the time that in any conflict between Thomas Cook and his son it was the son who held all the best cards. Thomas was nearly 70 and had already hinted at retirement. He had even, by 1878, commenced the building of a house in London Road, Leicester, for his home in retirement. The house was called "Thorncroft", and is now, 244 London Road. (It is currently used as the headquarters of the Leicestershire branch of the Red Cross, a use that would certainly have met with Thomas Cook's approval.) Even the building of this house, a substantial Italianate villa, proved to be a bone of contention between father and son for John accused his father of using the firm's money to pay for some of the bills of construction. For good measure the son claimed that he had urged retirement on his father as early as 1874 and said that he would allow him £1,000 p.a. or half the profits of the firm as long as he lived - on the face of it a not ungenerous allowance for those times.

The most wounding of the accusations (John claimed) was the matter concerning funds for the building of the Ludgate Circus headquarters. He stated that he had secured the land and was prepared to build on his own account with an agreement "that so long as I took care not to affect the credit of the firm I was to take what money I required". He claimed that his father actually took little interest in the development even though he tried to keep him informed and, although he agreed that he had never paid any interest on the money borrowed from the firm, he took no money in rent from the firm during the first four months of its occupation and also that he, personally, had paid £150 compensation to the new lessees of the old premises at 98 Fleet Street for whatever reason.

John conceded that he wrote and spoke plain English, adding, "I have also urged upon him (Thomas) that if instead of keeping to himself all kinds of erroneous ideas and dwelling upon them he would be frank and candid and say what he thinks to all concerned instead of behind their backs we should all be saved an immense amount of self-made trouble". He also wished for a family meeting to clear up matters but there is no reference to any such meeting taking place.

Matters had to come to a head and the firm could not continue successfully in such an atmosphere. John Mason Cook then forced the affair to a conclusion by a letter to his father, dated July 22nd, 1878, in which he claimed that the deed of partnership between them lapsed on December 30th, 1878, and did not provide for automatic renewal. Most decisively he added: "I will not sign or enter into any new arrangement for partnership with you upon any terms; all your recent letters prove the impossibility of us working together and my only hope now is that we both have health and strength to go through the work we are committed to ... and that we may both live to dissolve amicably". He refused to discuss the matter any further but denied that he wanted to deprive his father of his just rights adding: "As long as you live I want you to have half the profits of this business". Thomas Cook, knowing that at the age of 70 he had no hope of running the firm without the help of his son, capitulated. He gave away half his domain to his son in 1871 but according to John had proceeded as if he still controlled it all. Whatever his settlement Thomas could afford to live in some comfort in Leicester attended by adequate staff, was able to run a carriage with a coachman and able to maintain his own personal travel until he became physically incapable.

. . .

If Thomas Cook had ever given any hint of retirement in the mid-1870's his activities belie this. After his return from his tour of the world he continued to travel most extensively, particularly in the Middle East and kept up this sort of strenuous activity right to the moment of retirement. He found the annual visits to the Mediterranean region very beneficial to his health as he was beginning to suffer from bronchitis in the winter months in Britain. By October, 1874, he records that he had made nine visits to the eastern Mediterranean, six of them to Palestine and three trips up the Nile as far as the First Cataract With these visits and those to America he was away from home for very long periods. In earlier days this would have caused problems but after the entry of his son into the business such problems were progressively eased. He also entertained hopes of making a further circumnavigation of the globe. The Round the World Tour had indeed become an annual event in the firm's calendar but Thomas Cook himself was never to make the trip again. Others were to conduct parties on this strenuous exercise but he was to cross the Atlantic several more times. He visited

America in 1875 and again in 1876 which was the Centennial of the Declaration of Independence and which saw a large exhibition take place in Philadelphia. Thos. Cook & Son were appointed General Passenger Agents for the British Section of the Exhibition and Thomas Cook organised one of his Near Eastern tourist camps to be set up in the Exhibition Hall, presumably to encourage prospective US tourists to visit Egypt and Palestine under his auspices. He arranged for dragomans from the area to be in attendance. In full costume they must have appeared spectacular, including one Selim who had helped Stanley find the explorer Dr. Livingstone. This was an extremely busy year for Thomas Cook who visited the United States twice with only a three week break in between. During this break he even went on a Scottish tour where he revisited Iona taking with him a quantity of bread for the poor of the island.

Thomas Cook's health was no longer robust and this led him to cancel all thought of taking a tour round the world. It was announced in *The Excursionist* of August 3rd, 1876, that he "had desired, and intended, once more to circumnavigate the Globe but a severe bronchial attack, which prostrated him for nearly a month last winter, checked his ardour for an all-round trip". However, he returned from his second trip to America in December, 1876, "in excellent health" and decided to go East again in February, 1877. In fact he left on January 16th, barely 3 weeks after returning from America "determined to stay in Syria as long as he thinks necessary in the interests of travellers". Whilst there, trouble did erupt in Palestine and he was obliged to arrange for military escorts for his parties of travellers. He returned to England a few months later only to fall ill again. In May he suffered a severe attack of bronchitis which confined him to his room and "to the care of a couple of doctors and a contingent of family and domestic attendants for 3 weeks". He travelled to Eastbourne to convalesce and attributed his illness to the biting easterly winds in Leicester and London after his sojourn in Palestine. In July he was in Scotland, still not completely recovered, but in August he had apparently recovered sufficiently to conduct a party of tourists to Scandinavia. A great deal of his time in 1878 was occupied with an exhibition in Paris. He ran the Exhibition Boarding House as before and this proved to be his real swan-song. On April 1st, 1879 *The Excursionist* announced that Mr. John M. Cook would henceforth be "sole Managing Partner"

At the time of Thomas Cook's retirement the firm had grown to include 28 offices in Europe and the Near East, 6 in America and 1 in Australia. Its letter-head confidently stated: "Originators of the European Tourist Excursion Business. Established 1841. Specially appointed by His Royal Highness the Prince of Wales Sole Passenger Agents for the Royal British Commission in Vienna 1873, Philadelphia 1876 and Paris 1878. Sole Managing Agents of the Khedive Mail Steamers from Cairo (Egypt) to 1st and 2nd Cataracts of the Nile. Sole International Passenger Agents under special appointment by the Government Administration of the Italian State Railways".

VII
FAMILY MATTERS

Retirement would keep him busy! He continued to take an active interest in the promotion of Temperance and also in the General Baptist Church. His health was deteriorating causing him to seek warmer climes from time to time but always returning to his home town of Leicester.

With his daughter, Annie he was concerned with the baptist chapel in Archdeacon Lane. This was the poorer part of Leicester and gave the Cook family ample opportunity of service. Annie was active with the Sunday School and the young women's sewing group which met on the chapel premises on Saturday evenings. She was also fluent in French and had often accompanied her father on his tours of the Continent and he had relied on her to act as interpreter for him on may occasions. There was very obviously a strong bond between father and daughter. On one occasion she had even travelled with him to the Near East. It was from one of her Saturday evening sewing meetings that she returned home on November 6th, 1880, took supper with her parents and went upstairs for a bath before retiring to bed. It was about 11 p.m. when her father last spoke to her. She was never seen alive again but was discovered dead in her bath on Sunday morning, and an obituary was reported in *The Times*. It seems that a new patent 'instantaneous' gas water heater had been fitted to the bath:

> " ... and when the fatality occurred it had only been used three times. On a previous occasion when the deceased used the bath she complained to an intimate friend that when in the bath she lost consciousness and that she hardly knew how she recovered herself, as she felt on the verge on death. She, however, had not complained of this to her father or mother. On Saturday night Mr. Cook noticed a very disagreeable smell after the apparatus had been lighted. No more, however, was thought of the matter until Miss Cook was found dead in her bath. Dr. Henry Lankester, who was called, said he found evidence which showed that there had been an exceedingly high temperature in the room, and this together with the offensive odour from the gas apparatus,

induced syncope and Miss Cook was drowned. The room was fitted with electric bells, so that the deceased, had she had the power, could have called assistance at once."

At the inquest the jury returned a verdict of 'death by drowning'. There was, apparently, no attempt at the inquest to discover why the gas appliance had induced "syncope", fainting, in the deceased. The gas appliance was subsequently tested and found to be faulty. Apart from the doctor and Thomas Cook the other witness at the inquest was the "intimate friend" referred to in *The Times* report and can be identified as Mr. A. Akin Higgins. His emergence in the story gives added poignancy for he and Annie had been secretly engaged. The evidence he offered is reported and attributed in *The Leicester Chronicle* of November 13th. where he was described as residing at 28 Pocklingtons Walk, Leicester, and as being a "stock and share broker and general agent". He had in fact been in the employ of the firm of Thos. Cook & Son in Leicester when he met Annie and when their engagement had finally been revealed the prospect of gaining a brother-in-law from among his employees had filled John Mason Cook with considerable alarm. He had strongly opposed the intending marriage, threatening to terminate Higgins' employment with the firm (a threat which Higgins prevented from being carried out only by resigning). It is probable that John Cook saw any suitor for his sister's hand, and particularly one who was already in their employment, as a potential rival for control of the business. The inquest did not completely clear all the mystery surrounding Annie's death. The culprit was undoubtedly the appliance in the bathroom but the behaviour of both father and daughter just prior to her death is, to say the least, inexplicable. Rumours of suicide surfaced, arising from the unhappy circumstances of her engagement. As for Mr. Higgins, he is never heard of again.

Thomas and Marianne Cook grieved heavily over their daughter. Coupled with that grief must have been a large element of remorse for if Thomas Cook had taken prudent precautions it is more than likely that her untimely death would not have occurred. Marianne Cook never fully recovered from her devastating loss. Her daughter was undoubtedly a companion to her in her advancing years and she never had the same relationship with her daughter-in-law Emma. In the Leicestershire Records Office there is a large black book bearing the title, *In Memoriam - Autograph Letters of Condolence*, and it contains over 250 letters and cards to Thomas and Marianne Cook from sympathisers in Britain, America, Europe the Near East and India. There are letters from ministers of religion, hotel keepers, schools and societies as well as individuals. Some the Cook's hardly knew. One letter, in particular, is from Maurice Gostyuski writing from Crewe, Cheshire. In a neat hand he says:

> "Respected Sir, I apologise for taking the liberty of addressing you, being but an humble person, but I cannot satisfy my feelings without rendering you my deep sympathy in your great bereavement and now allow me to ask forgiveness for addressing you, hoping you will enjoy good health and long life. P.S. (I am) the Hairdress(er) who has been with you in Paris".

The funeral of Annie Cook took place the following Friday, November 12th and she was buried in Welford Road Cemetery, Leicester.

Thomas Cook lost no time in deciding how he would perpetuate the memory of Annie. In fact she had really given him the idea for opposite Archdeacon Lane Chapel was a vacant piece of land which she had often suggested to her father should be used to build a school-house. There were, apparently, about 900 children who attended Sunday School and she had tried to persuade him to finance the erection of a new building. He had always replied that he would do so only in conjunction with others if they were forthcoming. They were not, and after her death he resolved to go ahead on his own. *The Leicester Chronicle* published a letter from him on November 20th in which he "resolved to build a Memorial Hall, in which good works of various kinds may be done, both for the young and the aged". Thomas Cook later explained that the building was to be financed from the money he had set aside to provide for Annie had she survived him. She had died intestate and he believed that such a use of her inheritance would have met with her approval. Building work commenced and the Annie Elizabeth Cook Memorial Hall and Sunday School Room was officially opened on April 30th, 1882 at a public meeting held in the hall itself and attended by the Mayor of Leicester, Alderman Chambers, and many dignitaries of the town. In his own speech Thomas Cook outlined his purpose in building the hall and hoped that his friends in the Temperance

Society would also make use of the premises. Political parties were not to be excluded but it would not be let for "any object which was avowedly and decidedly hostile to the principles of the Christian religion". Needless to say, neither smoking tobacco nor the consumption of alcohol was to be allowed. The entire construction was paid for personally by Thomas Cook, the completed building then being handed over by him to Trustees. He had stoically refused any offers of financial help in the building but had been prepared to accept contributions for the establishment of a library. Mixed with his grief must undoubtedly have been a large element of remorse and from his writings at the time it is possible to see his heartfelt wish to spare no expense to perpetuate the memory of Annie on what he saw as a fitting scale. It is to be hoped that he found comfort from this act of generosity.

Archdeacon Lane Baptist Church was demolished in 1938 along with much slum clearance in the area. The Memorial Hall existed for another 30 years or so and was finally demolished in 1970. A marble bust of Annie Elizabeth, originally displayed in the Memorial Room of the hall, was saved, and is now in the custody of Buckminster Road Baptists, Leicester.

■ ■ ■

Life for the aging Marianne and Thomas must now have been a rather bleak existence. Annie had been a lively and intelligent young woman, It is also clear that Annie gave her parents the affection that appears to have been lacking in their son. Marianne Cook was 73 when her daughter died and never recovered from the shock. She had never been strong which may be why the Cooks did not have a larger family. She had however played an active part in the familiy business and it was she, with the help of Annie, who really organised the visitors who used the Exhibition Homes in London and Paris. One of her great interests towards the end of her life was the Baptist Mission in Rome which had been founded almost single-handedly by Thomas Cook in 1873 when he was on his way home from his tour around the world. Most of the facts concerning the life of Marianne Cook are provided by a pamphlet issued by Thomas Cook after her death and entitled *In Memoriam. Brief Notes on the Life, Labours, Sufferings and Death of Mrs. Marianne Cook*. In it he tells us that Marianne had frequently visited the Continent in the last twenty years of her life and had taken a deep interest in the Rome Mission where she subsequently liberally supported Mrs. Shaw in her effort to promote Mothers' Meetings and other social arrangements. In the same pamphlet we are given a picture of her last painful years. She had visited Italy 1882, had hoped to return the following spring but was too ill. She visited Bath and Bournemouth where she became very ill and with some difficulty was brought home to Leicester on February 19th, 1883.

> "For nearly three months she had to be carried from room to room; but in June she had so far recovered as to be able ... to occupy a through saloon carriage to Worthing ... Returning home early in July, she repeated her visit to Worthing in September ... She again returned to her home in the early part of October ... but her powers of endurance more rapidly declined ... and she calmly passed from Time to Eternity at six o'clock in the morning of the 8th of March" (1884).

Her funeral took place on Friday, March 14th, in the presence of most of the family although her son was away on business in Egypt with one of his own sons, Frank. She was buried in the same grave as Annie. The Mayor of Leicester also sent his apologies as did Rev. Charles Henry Spurgeon, founder of Spurgeon's College, the seminary for the training of Baptist ministers. Marianne Cook was clever enough to realise that after marriage her own fate depended entirely on that of her husband and she loyally supported him through all the difficulties and triumphs of their lives together. Little has come down to us of the private relationship between husband and wife. Few letters survive and those which do certainly show an affection and respect, even devotion, but expressed in a controlled and undemonstrative style so typical of the age which worshipped respectability. If Thomas mourned for Annie more than for his wife then this is understandable for her untimely death was one that was totally avoidable.

. . .

Thomas Cook's final years were very lonely ones. He had lost the two people closest to him, and although he remained on speaking terms with his son, there was never a close relationship between them.

Albert Bishop wrote of his memories of Thomas Cook to Thomas Budge written in 1952:

"I remember Mr. Cook chiefly as an old man, of course. His kind benevolent face was usually either placid or smiling and no doubt to my eyes when I first knew him he seemed older than he really was. He used on Sundays to sit in the back seat of Archdeacon Lane Chapel and he had a habit of putting his hands together and twirling his thumbs over one another during the whole time he was listening to the sermon. I have no memory of his doing it at other times though he may have done so. He was a regular attendant on Sundays and after he went to live at Thorncroft, he had a closed-in carriage, something like a glorified small bus (without top seats of course), with a seat down each side. The cushions were covered with blue cloth and when Mr. Cook called at our house to take Mother down to chapel, as he sometimes did, I used occasionally to get a ride, and when this happened, I felt myself to be a very grand and fortunate person ... As a family we were always invited up to Thorncroft for Christmas Day. Thorncroft situated on London Road was then on the outskirts of Leicester and to my brother and me it seemed a very large and almost palatial abode. The front door gave onto a big square Hall round which were the doors opening into the Dining, Breakfast, Drawing Rooms and Library. There was also a door leading to the Kitchen premises. A wide staircase led up to a balcony constructed round the Hall and both the Hall and balcony were lit by a big roof light. All the bedrooms opened off this balcony. Altogether it was, I think, a commodious, well-planned and well-built house of good sound red brick. Mr. Cook loved to have his friends round him at the Festive Season. There was a long table in the Dining Room, generally full to capacity on Christmas Day. My father was always given the job of carving the turkey (of prodigious size) at one end of the table and generally one of the Mason family was at the other end to carve the huge sirloin of beef. Father had the worst of it as everyone seemed to prefer turkey. We boys used afterwards to be allowed to play at puss-in-the-corner in the Hall with some of the younger guests and I seem to remember in the early days Mr. Cook coming out of the Drawing Room to watch benevolently as we enjoyed our game ..."

Retirement gave Thomas Cook the opportunity to concentrate on the causes which were so close to his heart without the risk of incurring the displeasure of his son and business partner. Although progressively failing in health he remained as active as possible in the cause which had led him into his illustrious career. His religious convictions had led him to temperance and this in turn had, by one event in 1841, opened his fertile imagination to the enormous possibilities of organising travel. He was well enough to take part in the Jubilee of the Market Harborough Temperance Society in 1886. The celebrations, marking the 50th anniversary of the emergence of temperance in Leicestershire began with a meeting in the Temperance Hall, Leicester, on Saturday, November 13th, when Thomas Cook, as President of the Leicester Temperance Society, took the Chair.

Although he no longer was able to organise parties of travellers his own personal travel continued for several years. He was usually accompanied by a friend, Mr. Glasgow, who travelled with him to Italy in 1884, just after Marianne's death. The following year, 1885, he made what was to prove his last visit to America, in 1886 the two of them visited Scotland and in 1888 Thomas Cook persuaded his son to allow him to travel once more to the Nile and Palestine. Visits to various parts of England were also included and it was on one of these, to Worthing in May, 1890, that he wrote, with Mr. Glasgow acting as "a friendly amanuensis" because of "darkened windows which forbid all personal writing", of his last great act of generosity. He decided to build, at his own expense, at Melbourne, his birthplace, a group of cottages together with a mission hall and then hand over the premises to trustees. In this way hoped to perpetuate the memory of his family, his career and his connection with the General Baptist Church. Thomas Cook also intended to keep two residences "arranged and furnished for the temporary use of the Founder of the buildings, and friends whom he may invite; and he has it in contemplation to give free accommodation to Ministers and their Wives who have but limited means for recreation and rest, on condition that they assist in the services of the Mission Hall".

The set of buildings still stands forming three sides of a quadrangle opening on to High Street, Melbourne. They are still occupied and remain in the hands of Trustees. The mission hall is no longer used for its original purpose but is very much in community use. The tablets fixed to the walls by Thomas Cook in July, 1890 are still there, one of them referring to the cottages set aside for his own use as a "House of Call". There is, in addition, a tablet fixed to the wall of the mission hall in more recent times commemorating his birth in Quick Close, a mere stone's throw from the cottages.

. . .

In 1891 the firm of Thos. Cook & Son reached its 50th anniversary and the occasion was marked by the publication of its first history, *The Business of Travel* by W. Fraser Rae. There was also a dinner held in the Guildhall in London but Thomas Cook was unable to make the journey to London from Leicester to attend the celebrations. He was spending much of his time, as he said, dreaming of excursions long past.

John Mason Cook presided at the dinner and spoke of his father's present frailty, adding that when he had last spoken to him he did not recognise his, (John's) voice. Facts given at the Guildhall by John Mason Cook revealed how much the firm had grown. "In 1865", he declared, "the whole personnel of the business consisted of Thomas Cook, myself, two assistants and one messenger ... In 1890 we had a staff of 1,714 permanent salaried members. In addition it required 978 persons, chiefly Arabs, to work our business in Egypt and Palestine ... To regulate this business, and enable us to conduct it in all parts of the globe we have 45 distinct banking accounts; and either as our own property or under rental or lease we have 84 offices worked by salaried staff of the firm, and in addition 85 agencies". This was a story of consolidation indeed. Many distinguished members of late Victorian society were included in the guest list for the dinner. Some, inevitably, could not attend and sent their apologies. John Mason Cook read a portion of one of the letters to the assembled guests. It had been sent from Hawarden Castle and was dated July 9th 1891.

> "Dear Sir,
>
> Until the heavy affliction befell me at the close of last week, although I have been long prohibited from attending public dinners, I had a vain hope of being medically permitted to make yours an exception, and to avail myself of your very kind invitation. This has now gone by; but I cannot satisfy myself even at this moment with a merely formal negative. I desire simply to say that I do not regard your festival as a mere celebration of commercial success, and of the active qualities which produce it. I conceive that the idea which your house was, I believe, the first to conceive and patiently to work out, has distinctly placed you in the rank of public benefactors; and the competitors who have sprung or may yet spring up around you are so many additional witnesses to the real greatness of the service you have rendered.
>
> With warm, good wishes for the coming and for every occasion that concerns you, I remain your very faithful and obedient servant."
>
> W. E. GLADSTONE.

■ ■ ■

Thomas Cook was to live just one more year after receiving this accolade from the great Victorian statesman.

He left very little money - scarcely £2, 500. The business was of course already in the hands of his son John, who died a wealthy man seven years later. Personal effects were inherited by his grandchildren and his home in Leicester was sold to a member of the Ellis family which had played such an important part in his career.

EPILOGUE

In November, 1834, Sir Robert Peel was summoned back to London from Italy to become prime minister. The journey took twelve days to complete. When Thomas Cook died in 1892 the journey could be completed in 2 days, and in reasonable comfort with first-class railway carriages and Channel crossings by steamer.

On his own admission he was not very interested in railways but he was called upon to organise trips between 1841 and 1845. His work for the temperance movement brought the need to travel and we see how that need pursuaded him that the railways could serve the movement. From this developed a business which gave the opportunity to travel to thousands of people who otherwise could not afford to do so. His formula for success was a simple one: he was able to provide bespoke travel for those who needed it. As a printer he had been engaged in the oldest, and for centuries the only, mass production industry. Engaging a special train was very little different in conception from preparing a plate for use on a printing machine. The more copies that were run off, to capacity, the cheaper each individual copy became, the large bulk of the cost being in the setting-up. The more people boarding a train, to capacity, the cheaper the cost of transporting each individual traveller, the expense of running an empty train being very little different from running a full one. His genius was in being able to find the passengers better than anyone else at the time. The nineteenth century also saw the rise both in the economic and political spheres, of the middle classes. Thomas Cook's career reflected this and he himself became prosperous middle class from his very humble beginnings. Politics never really interested him. The nearest he came to that sort of activity was his interest in the Anti-Corn Law League of the 1840's but he was much more interested in the price of bread than power.

Thomas Cook is rare in that he came from the class whom he tried to help, and in the words of W. E. Gladstone his service to the nation make it fitting that he be placed "in the rank of public benefactors".

BIBLIOGRAPHY

Thomas J. Budge	Melbourne Baptists The Carey Kingsgate Press, 1951
Thomas Cook	A Memoir of Samuel Deacon Thomas Cook, 1888
A. Dawson Burns	Temperance History National Temperance Publication Depot, 1889
I. C. Ellis	Records of Nineteenth Century Leicester Privately Printed 1935
F. Ferneyhough	The Liverpool and Manchester Railway 1830 - 1980 R. Hale, 1980
J. R. Godfrey	Historic Memorials of Barton and Melbourne Buck, Winks & Son, Leicester, 1891
Marilyn Palmer	Framework Knitting Shire Publications Ltd, 1984
A. Temple Patterson	Radical Leicester Leicester University College, 1954
John Pudney	The Thomas Cook Story Michael Joseph, 1953
W. Fraser Rae	The Business of Travel Thos. Cook & Son, 1891
Clement Stretton	The History of the Midland Railway Methuen, 1901
Edmund Swinglehurst	Romantic Journey Pica Editions, 1974
R. H. G. Thomas	The Liverpool and Manchester Railway A. Reid, Newcastle-on-Tyne, 1915
R. A. Williams	The London and South Western Railway David and Charles, Newton Abbot, 1968

The Victoria County History